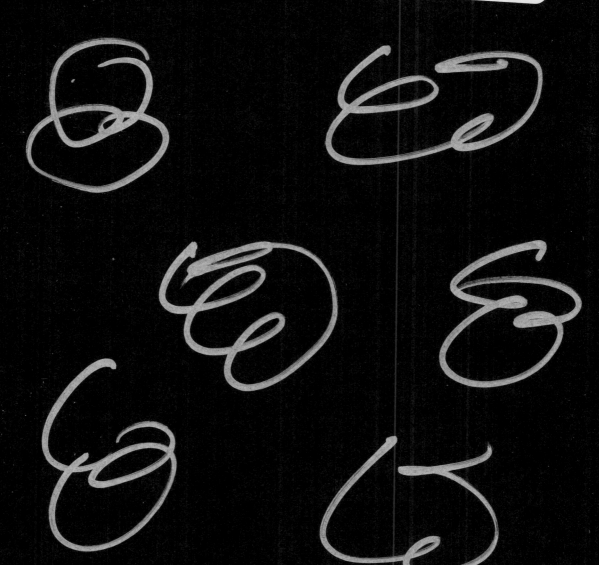

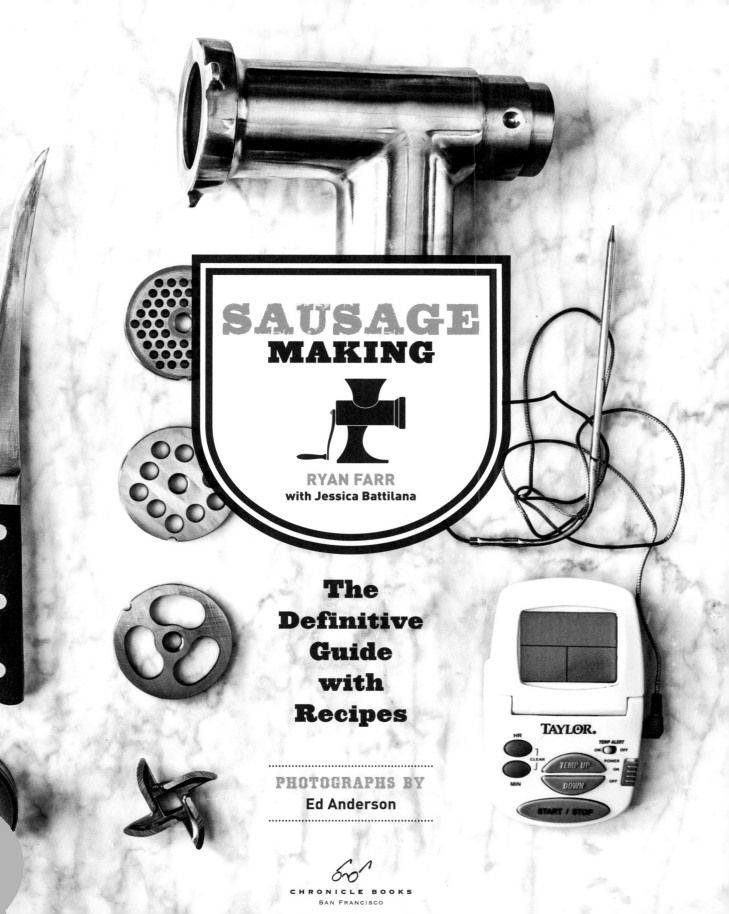

SAUSAGE MAKING

RYAN FARR

with Jessica Battilana

The Definitive Guide with Recipes

PHOTOGRAPHS BY

Ed Anderson

CHRONICLE BOOKS

SAN FRANCISCO

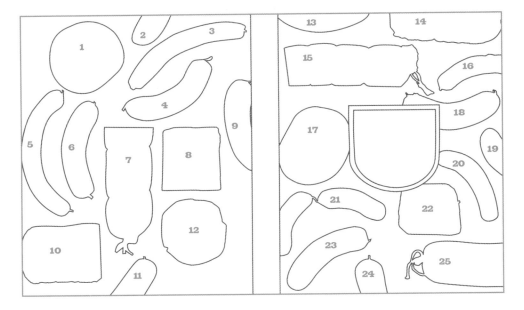

1. Blood Bologna
2. Butcher's Sausage
3. The Kermit
4. Smoked Trout and Pork Sausage
5. Venison and Juniper Sausage
6. Lao Sausage
7. Liverwurst
8. Truffled Boudin en Croute
9. Bacon, Cheddar, and Beef Links
10. Veal, Sweetbreads, and Morels en Croute
11. Cajun Boudin
12. Stinky Taleggio Crepinette

13. Guinea Hen and Kimchee Links
14. Chicken and Egg Galantine
15. Summer Sausage
16. Merguez
17. Bierwurst
18. Boudin Noir with Winter Fruit
19. Smoked Polish Sausage
20. Chorizo
21. Maple-Bacon Breakfast Sausage
22. Duck Confit and Cherry Terrine
23. Linguiça
24. Scottish White Pudding
25. Duck Cotechino

Library of Congress Cataloging-in-Publication Data:
Farr, Ryan.
 Sausage Making: the definitive guide with recipes/ Ryan Farr.
  pages cm
 Includes index.
 ISBN 978-1-4521-0178-1 (alk. paper)
1. Sausages. I. Title.

TS1974.S3F37 2014
641.3'6—dc23

2013026813

Manufactured in China

FSC
www.fsc.org

MIX
Paper from responsible sources
FSC® C008047

Designed by VANESSA DINA
Typesetting by HAPPENSTANCE TYPE-O-RAMA

10 9 8 7 6 5 4 3 2 1

Chronicle Books LLC
680 Second Street
San Francisco, California 94107
www.chroniclebooks.com

To my wife, Cesalee, my son, Tanner,
and my daughter, Scarlett

CONTENTS

ACKNOWLEDGMENTS

To Cesalee: You make being an amazing mom and wife look so easy. I am humbled by you and at my best when we are together.

To Tanner and Scarlett: Watching you grow up is the greatest gift I could ever receive. I will always support you and your dreams, as you are supporting mine.

To my amazing family: Mom, Dad, Cathleen, Lauren, Chelsea, Caela, Carolyn, Hob, and all my aunts, uncles, and cousins, we share so many great memories that all start in the kitchen.

To all the hard-working, ass-kicking folks who have helped build 4505 Meats: Because of you, we are not only a meat company, we are a family. Special thanks to Dan, Kyle, Claire, Gerrardo, Thomas, Emma, Andrew, Jose, Kent, and Cole. Without you this book wouldn't have been possible. Thank you.

To Cole Mayfield: Your recipe-testing skills and ability to fix all broken things is a skill few possess. You are a great man, sir. Thank you. Kent Schoberle, not only can you butcher and teach whole animal butchery skillfully, your graphic contributions to this book and 4505 Meats have taken our game to the next level. Thank you, my friend.

To Jessica Battilana: We have created a book to be proud of. From the beginning vision to the very end you have been a delight to work with.

To Lorena Jones, Vanessa Dina, Doug Ogan, Elizabeth Smith, Steve Kim, Peter Perez, David Hawk, and the whole talented team at Chronicle Books: You are known for creating exquisite books and this one is an excellent example.

To Ed Anderson: Your ability to capture beauty in something like sausage making is a true talent.

To Carole Bidnick: Thank you for the continued guidance and all your hard work. You are a great friend and agent.

To Bruce Aidells: Thank you for continuing to mentor me in all things meaty and, unknowingly, in life, too. You are the undisputed Sausage King.

To my Denver friends who have supported me from day one: Some of my best memories are of grilling sausages and steaks in our backyards. It all started with you and I love you all.

To all the amazing customers who support us every day: Without you and your love for sausage, it would be a sad, sausageless world.

Of course this only scratches the surface of all the people who have supported me on my journey leading up to today. Thank you all from the bottom of my heart.

INTRODUCTION

As a butcher and a chef, I am passionate about whole-animal utilization. That philosophy was the guiding principle behind my first book, *Whole Beast Butchery*, which teaches how to butcher an entire animal and how to best utilize and cook the resulting cuts.

So it only seemed fitting that my second book be devoted to sausage, which originated as a way for butchers to turn odds, ends, and non-prime cuts of meat into something incredibly satisfying and delicious. When I started my business, 4505 Meats, five years ago, the first product that we made were our *chicharrones*—light, crunchy pork rinds that immediately developed a cult following. The second product I brought to market was hot dogs. In the early days, my process for making the hot dogs was, frankly, a bit of a disaster. I was working in several rented kitchens, so I'd butcher and grind the meat for the hot dogs in one kitchen, then drive the ground meat across town to a second kitchen, where there was a commercial-grade mixer, to mix the meat. Then I'd drive the mixed meat across town again, back to the first kitchen, to stuff and smoke the dogs.

It was completely inefficient, and the problem only worsened as the hot dogs became more popular. What I would have given to have a book like this when I was first starting out! Well, that, and an extra 48 hours in every week.

Part of the reason that I started making hot dogs was because most of the commercially available dogs on the American market were not something I wanted to eat or feed my family. Made with subpar meat and flavored with liquid smoke, the average hot dog is a very sad sausage. I wanted to make a dog that was snappy and juicy, with a real smoky flavor, made from sustainably raised meat.

Sausages have gotten a bad reputation. Though historically they were made with care, once mass-produced factory sausages became the norm, the quality of commercially available links suffered. Questions about what exactly was inside that casing caused many to shy away from purchasing and eating them.

So I set out to make sausages that I was proud to serve, sausages that I would feed my children, sausages that contained ingredients that were both pronounceable and that came from farms that I knew and respected. Not only did I enjoy coming up with new varieties, but I also was happy to restore integrity to well-known sausages, like bratwurst (see page 74) and chorizo (see page 56).

With over a decade of experience in sausage, using my classical culinary training and good sourcing practices, I was able to create some really great sausage, finding more ways to utilize the whole animals that I was getting.

I created master ratios for different textures of sausage: coarse, firm, soft, and smooth. With those ratios in hand, I started to riff on flavor combinations, inspired by fruits and vegetables I'd find at the market, meat I had on hand, or time-honored pairings.

The fundamentals of sausage making are the same, though, whether you are crafting a coarse Italian-style sausage (see page 64) or a smooth boudin blanc (see page 122), and there are techniques for grinding and mixing the meat, methods for stuffing the sausage meat into casings, and instructions for twisting those casings into links that are almost universal, no matter what type of sausage you're making. The first part of this book explains all the technical aspects of sausage making, from what tools you should have to how to successfully transform raw meat into finished, cased sausage. Before you attempt any of the recipes you should read the following primer and chapter 1 carefully, as every recipe relies on that knowledge. There is also information about the various ways to cook your sausages, from grilling to poaching to smoking. Sausage should be treated with as much care as any cut of meat, and careful cooking ensures that the finished product will be juicy and delicious.

The rest of the book is divided into chapters based on what texture of sausage you'd like to make. Each chapter begins with the master ratio for that texture, so if you have some meat scraps on hand or are hit with some inspiration, you can create your own recipe, or you can simply follow the recipes that I've created. They make relatively small batches, so they're appropriate for a home cook, but the recipes can be easily multiplied if you'd like to make a bigger batch.

The overall goal of this book is to restore glory to the humble sausage; to inspire you to use every part of the animal to create sausages that are truly wonderful, and to enjoy the process of making them.

A SAUSAGE PRIMER

· ·

At its most basic, sausage is a pretty simple product: just ground meat and fat combined with salt, spices, and liquid, formed into patties or stuffed into casings. Sausage is a handy way to utilize meat scraps efficiently, but it has the added benefit of being totally delicious.

I've created dozens of different varieties of sausage at 4505 Meats, from boudin blanc studded with cubes of fresh nectarine to coarse, spicy lamb merguez links to traditional breakfast sausage flavored with maple syrup and sage.

When I set out to make a new sausage, I think first about the texture of the final product, which is why I've organized this book by texture. Do I want a smooth sausage, with a texture like a hot dog? Or am I looking to make something that has a coarse, rustic texture, like chorizo? Would I prefer a soft sausage with a fluffy texture, such as a boudin blanc, or something firm, like a smoked linguiça?

The texture of a sausage is determined by the amount of meat, fat, and liquid that it contains and how the ingredients are combined. For each of the four textures (coarse, smooth, soft, and firm) there is a master ratio, an equation that can be adjusted based on how much sausage I want to end up with or how much meat I have to use up.

Though the recipes in the book don't require an understanding of these master ratios, which are presented at the start of each chapter, they're helpful if you want to create your own recipes, experiment with different flavor combinations, or vary the type of meat you're using. You'll see that I've given you formulas for each recipe that show the ratios of every ingredient as a percentage of the total, in addition to U.S. measurements. The formulas are based on the yields of the recipes in grams and enable you to accurately scale the recipe up (or down) so you will able to make sausages for a crowd as easily and as successfully as you would make a single batch.

In the interest of preventing waste and making these recipes user-friendly, I've made them completely adaptable, based on the weight of the meat being prepared. All that's required if you want to maintain the consistency of the recipe is to multiply the percentage of the ingredient by the total weight of the recipe in grams. This formula is always based on the yield of the recipe in grams. The process is far more intuitive when working in grams, but I've also included volume measurements (cups and tablespoons), as well as the percentages for each ingredient. It works like this:

**Desired weight of recipe in grams
× % of ingredient = weight of ingredient**

**Example: Recipe yields 1,000 grams
× 10% salt = 100 grams of salt**

(Remember: to convert a percentage into a decimal, shift the decimal point two spots to the left (10% = 0.10). This will make your calculations much easier.)

Tools of the Trade

There are not a lot of necessary tools for sausage making, but the few that you do need are critical for the success of your finished product. Calculating the ingredients for a recipe, weighing carefully, grinding cleanly, and proper stuffing are essential parts of making great sausage. Always make sure your tools are clean and in good working order before you begin.

CALCULATOR

A standard calculator is an invaluable tool for home sausage making. It's especially key when you start developing your own recipes, or if you are trying to utilize trim from butchering a whole animal.

CASINGS AND CAUL FAT

By weight, casings are the most expensive ingredient in sausage making. Almost without exception, natural casings are hand-cleaned and sold by the hank, which is a measurement of length. Natural casings come packed in either salt or in brine; before using they should be soaked in cold water for 24 to 48 hours, refreshing the water periodically. Casings will keep, packed in salt and refrigerated, for up to a year; rinse them well before using. Just before stuffing, run warm water through the casings. You can also purchase ready-to-stuff casings on flow line tubes, which are plastic tubes onto which the casings have been threaded, making it easier to transfer the casing to the nose of the stuffer; these are typically sold packed in brine and still need to be soaked overnight before using.

Hog casings are the small intestine of the animal and can be purchased in multiple sizes. They're typically used for country-style linked sausage, bratwurst, and any other sausages with a diameter larger than a hot dog.

Sheep casings are thinner than hog casings and come in different grades and sizes. We typically use what is known as "frankfurter size," which isn't the largest but is the most common, popular size. We use only Grade A sheep casings, which have fewer holes; these are the casings most typically used for hot dogs and will give you a snappier sausage than B- or C-grade casings.

Beef casings come in three sizes: beef round, the small intestine of the animal; beef middle, the large intestine of the animal; and beef bung, which is the largest of the three. Beef rounds are only slightly smaller than middles and can be substituted for each another; I use the middles as casings for summer sausage and liverwurst. Middles are most frequently used for dried salami. The bung is used to case mortadella and bologna. Beef casings are thicker and more resilient than hog or sheep casings, making them a good choice for coarse sausage that will be smoked or dried. They have a pronounced aroma and should be soaked for several days before using.

Synthetic casings, made of collagen, are also available. They are sold by the piece and adhere nicely to the meat within, making them a good choice for meat sticks. Store in a resealable bag in a dry place. Do not pack them in salt or put them in salt brine, which will cause them to melt.

Caul fat can also be used in place of casings. Derived from the stomach lining of cows, sheep, and pigs, this lacy membrane has a web of fat strands that dissolve when the caul fat is heated, basting the enclosed meat as it cooks. Caul fat is usually sold frozen. To leach out any impurities, soak it in water, refrigerated, changing the water frequently, until the caul fat is white, 24 to 48 hours.

GRINDER

Buying preground meat is scary. In this day and age, I don't suggest that anyone do it, unless you know where it's coming from and have a butcher you trust. A better solution is to invest in a grinder and grind your meat yourself, so you know exactly what's going into your grind.

If you're an occasional sausage maker, the grinder attachment available for KitchenAid stand mixers is a good option. You can get the blades and dies sharpened by a knife sharpener; I recommend buying additional blades and dies if you plan to make a lot of sausage so that you always have a sharp set. If you grind your meat using a dull blade, not only will the meat heat up as the blade slowly grinds it, it will also pulverize the cell structure of the meat. This makes it more difficult to suspend fat in the meat, meaning that you'll never get that beautiful emulsification of fat and meat that makes for a juicy, succulent sausage. Instead, you'll be contending with a grainy, greasy sausage.

If you're planning to make a lot of sausage (or burgers, or anything else with ground meat) I suggest investing in a tabletop grinder with a 350- to 800-watt motor. A grinder of this type has the torque and power behind it to quickly and cleanly grind your meat. This type of grinder will set you back a few hundred dollars, but it's a worthy investment.

SAUSAGE PRICKER

With a small knife on one end and a multiprong pricker on the other, this is a useful all-in-one tool for removing air pockets from cased sausages and separating links. In our kitchen we refer to it as the "magic wand."

SAUSAGE STUFFER

A sausage stuffer is an essential tool for sausage making. At the simpler end are the horizontal stuffers, often made of cast iron, that can be bolted to your countertop. They are inexpensive but cumbersome to use. I prefer vertical, stainless-steel canister-style stuffers. Like horizontal stuffers, they are hand-cranked, but the design is better and they are easier to use. They are also more expensive and larger; the smallest model is intended for a 5-lb/2.3-kg batch of sausage.

In addition to the grinder attachment, Kitchen-Aid also sells a stuffing attachment compatible with the stand mixers, but I find it difficult to use, particularly for larger batches.

SCALE

In our kitchen we have a variety of scales, including hanging scales that we use to weigh whole sides of beef. But at home, a small, inexpensive digital scale is all you really need. Purchase one that can measure both grams and ounces and that, at minimum, can hold up to 10 lb/4.5 kg.

THERMOMETER

You can't make a hot dog with hot meat: a thermometer is a critical tool for successful sausage making. You cannot make quality sausage without one. It's essential that you monitor the temperature of your raw ingredients when you're making your sausage, but equally important that you cook your sausage to the perfect degree of doneness, just as you would a steak or piece of chicken.

If you habitually cut into a piece of meat as it cooks to check its doneness, I'm speaking to you: buy a thermometer. I use a laser thermometer to monitor the temperature of my raw ingredients and a probe thermometer to check the internal temperature of cooked sausage. Improper temperatures in both the preparation and the cooking of sausage leads to a disappointing finished product.

Salt and Cure

Salt is a critical ingredient in sausage making. Not only is it necessary for flavor, it also aids in the preservation of the sausage. I prefer to use a fine sea salt, such as La Baleine brand, which has a nice, clean flavor and disperses evenly through the sausage.

Curing salts are another essential ingredient, comprising sodium nitrite or nitrate (or both) and salt. Both nitrate and nitrite are converted to nitric oxide by microorganisms and combine with the meat pigment myoglobin to give the cured meat a pink color. But the main reason that curing salts are used is to prevent the growth of botulism-producing organisms that might otherwise thrive, and to retard rancidity. In large quantities, both nitrite and nitrate are toxic to humans. For that reason, never use more curing salts than called for in a recipe. Here are the most commonly used cures:

INSTA CURE NO. 1. Also known as pink salt, this cure is used for fresh sausage or cured, cooked sausages, and contains a mixture of sodium nitrite and salt, which both preserves the sausage and helps it retain its pink color.

INSTA CURE NO. 2. Typically used for dried sausages that are cured but not cooked, such as pepperoni, Cure No. 2 contains both sodium nitrite and sodium nitrate. Because these dried sausages are never heated, the nitrate breaks down slowly like a time-release capsule, curing the meat over an extended period of time.

NATURAL CURE. Marketed as an alternative to synthetically produced curing salts, celery juice powder contains naturally occurring, vegetable-derived nitrites and nitrates that, like the synthetic versions, convert into nitric oxide. The USDA currently does not recognize naturally occurring nitrites and nitrates as an effective curing agent for meat; therefore products made with natural cure must be labeled as uncured. If replacing Insta Cure No. 1 with natural cure, you need to multiply the amount of Insta Cure No. 1 by 2.5.

Both Insta Cure No. 1 and Cure No. 2, as well as celery juice powder, are available at specialty butcher shops and online.

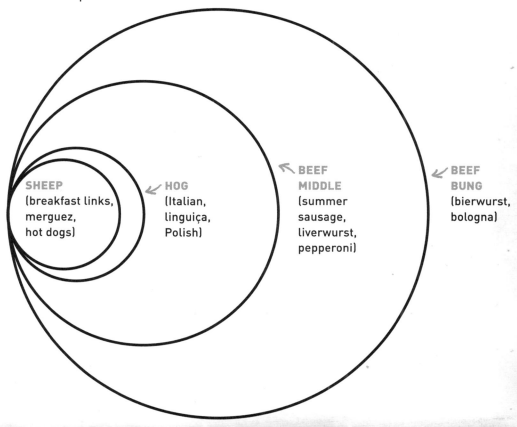

SHEEP
(breakfast links, merguez, hot dogs)

HOG
(Italian, linguiça, Polish)

BEEF MIDDLE
(summer sausage, liverwurst, pepperoni)

BEEF BUNG
(bierwurst, bologna)

CHAPTER 1

MEAT, SALT, FAT, AND TECHNIQUE

pork skin

bacon

hog casing

salt

leaf fat

beef middles

caul fat

back fat

beef chuck

pork shoulder steak

Sausage is an emulsification of meat, fat, and liquid, and it's the relative proportion of these ingredients that determines the texture of the sausage. When protein (ground meat) and liquid are combined, the mixture forms a sticky paste, called *farce*, that can readily absorb fat.

In general, the lean-to-fat ratio remains the same no matter what type or texture of sausage you are making. It's the amount of added liquid, and how the meat mixture is handled, that determines the final texture of the sausage.

Selecting Meat and Fat for Sausage

Though almost any kind of meat or seafood can be used in sausage, the most flavorful sausages have a lean-to-fat ratio of approximately 75 percent lean to 25 percent fat. Sausage needs fat to be flavorful, and that fat can come from the cuts of meat that you choose, such as well-marbled pork shoulder, or can be added in separately to supplement leaner protein like rabbit or pork leg. Sausage is a fabulous way to utilize meat scraps (especially useful if you are butchering a whole animal) and excellent sausage is made from cuts of meat that are less expensive. While each recipe in the book will suggest a particular cut of meat, the following meat and fat information is especially useful if you're utilizing a whole animal or want to make sausage using meat you have on hand.

BEEF

LEAN. Beef neck (without fat cap), round, plate meat, and shank are about 90 to 95 percent lean and are great cuts for sausage because they are high in protein. More liquid (and in turn, more fat) can be added to a cut that is high in protein, resulting in a juicy, flavorful sausage. These cuts are primarily used in smooth and puréed sausages.

MODERATE. Beef chuck and sirloin are about 80 percent lean and can also be used to make sausage, though because these muscles typically have between 15 and 20 percent intramuscular fat, you have to be mindful of the amount of fat and water that you add to the sausage. Add too much additional fat and water and you'll end up breaking the emulsification, resulting in grainy, dry sausage that leaks grease when you cut into it. That said, these cuts do make excellent sausage, particularly of the coarse variety.

FATTY. Beef from the flank section, short ribs, brisket, and fatty trim meat have between 40 and 60 percent fat. These muscles are best used as additions to lean and moderate beef cuts to boost the flavor and make the texture silkier, but are too fatty to be used on their own to make sausage.

PORK

MODERATE. Pork shoulder is approximately 75 percent lean and is a great go-to muscle for sausage. It can be used on its own, or you can make an especially succulent sausage with the addition of up to 5 percent additional fat.

LEAN. Sirloin and leg are both leaner cuts of pork, about 95 percent lean, and are a good addition to any fatty blend of sausage farce. If you're butchering a whole animal, remove the chops, ham, shoulder, and belly. The remaining trim is very fatty, but when used in combination with the sirloin and 30 percent of the leg you'll end up with a blend that is about 75 percent lean, 25 percent fat, ideal for sausage (and a great use of meat scraps).

FATTY. The belly is the fattiest part of the pig, about 50 percent fat, 50 percent lean, and therefore is not good for sausage on its own. This cut should be used in combination with leaner cuts of meat, where it adds flavor and succulence. Pork back fat and bacon are also great additions to sausage.

PORK SKIN. Collagen-rich pork skin gives sausage a silky texture and acts as a vehicle for flavor, though has little flavor of its own. To make it edible, the skin must first be boiled in water until very tender, then cooled completely before it is ground. Once cooked, and the skin is fully chilled and ground, it can be mixed into the sausage farce; when the sausage is heated, the skin dissolves and gives the sausage a pleasing finger-licking quality. If puréed with water while still warm, pork skin can be used as an emulsifying agent.

LAMB

MODERATE. Lamb has moderate fat content, about 80 percent. You can use the entire animal, except for the chops, to make sausage. A combination of leg and belly makes for a particularly good sausage; lamb neck, which comprises small muscles held together by pockets of fat, is also a choice cut. I generally use lamb to make coarse, highly seasoned sausages, such as Merguez (page 62); if making a smooth lamb sausage, like the lamb wieners on page 126, I'll add some lean beef, extra liquid, and fat to aid the emulsification.

GOAT

Goat meat is about 85 percent lean, so sausages made with goat meat will need additional fat and liquid added in order to achieve a moist, flavorful sausage.

CHICKEN

Skin-on chicken thighs are about 80 percent lean and are great for making smooth sausages. It's easy to emulsify the meat without adding additional fat, but you can also add some (often in the form of egg yolks or cream) without worrying about the emulsification breaking, as the meat is high in protein. The skin, which is all fat, also contributes a lot of good flavor. Skinless chicken thighs can also be used, but because they are 95 percent lean, additional fat, chicken or otherwise, must be added to achieve the correct ratio of 75 percent lean and 25 percent fat. I don't recommend making sausage with chicken breasts, as they are too lean and fibrous.

RABBIT

I suggest using rabbit shoulder, leg, belly, and trim for sausage and saving the loin for another use, as it's very lean. If you're working with a whole animal, add in the clusters of fat around the kidneys, or supplement the meat with pork fat, bacon, or cream to make an especially juicy sausage.

FISH AND SHELLFISH

Flaky fish, such as cod, halibut, and sturgeon are good for sausage, though because they are relatively lean, additional fat needs to be added, such as eggs or cream. Scallops are also great for seafood sausage.

FROG

You can treat frog meat the same way that you treat fish. It is too delicate to grind so it's best to hand-chop the meat. Blend it with eggs and cream as you would a fish sausage.

EGG

Egg whites are very lean but extremely high in protein, so they are an excellent emulsifying agent and can be used in puréed sausages. Whole eggs have more fat; they too act as emulsifying agents but also add richness and creaminess to the finished sausage.

HEAVY CREAM

I use heavy cream in place of water or other liquids to add fat and flavor to rich, fluffy sausages like Foie Gras Boudin Blanc (page 122) and Chicken-Beer Sausage (page 120).

LIVER AND OFFAL

There's not a lot of fat in liver and it is high in protein, but it doesn't have the same liquid-holding properties as lean pork or beef, and therefore is most commonly used in conjunction with these meats, along with additional fat and eggs or cream. Liver is good as a supporting ingredient, as it contributes a lot of flavor. Heart and kidneys are a nice addition. Heart contains some fat (about 5 percent by weight) but kidneys are very lean.

NATURAL FILLERS

Bread and rice are both added to sausages as filler, to stretch a small amount of meat further. Cajun-style boudin sausage (see page 98) often contains rice, which gives the sausage a nice texture. Bread is a great binder and can be used in place of flour, because it also adds flavor.

Step-by-Step Master Technique

What follows is a complete guide to making sausage, beginning with raw meat and ending with finished links. This process is essentially the same no matter what type of sausage you are making, and we cross-reference it throughout the book.

GRINDING

STEP 1: Cut the meat into easy-to-handle pieces. Trim any sinew, blood clots, bone fragments, and glands—anything that you don't want to eat—from the meat and fat and cut the meat into 1-in/2.5-cm cubes (or a size slightly smaller than the opening of your meat grinder). Keep your workstation and tools clean to avoid cross-contamination.

STEP 2: Open-freeze the meat. Spread it in a single layer on a rimmed baking sheet or dinner plate and place in the freezer, uncovered, for 30 to 60 minutes, until the surface of the meat is crunchy to the touch and the interior is very cold but not frozen solid.

Place the grinder and dies in the refrigerator and refrigerate until very cold (don't put in the freezer to chill, or the meat will stick to the grinder).

Maintaining the best temperature is critical in sausage making; if your ingredients are well chilled, they will combine better and more easily. Cleanly ground meat will absorb more liquid and more fat, both of which are essential to flavorful sausage.

STEP 3: Nest an empty bowl in a larger bowl filled with ice and assemble the clean, chilled grinder. We use a ³⁄₁₆-in/4-mm die for every sausage, unless otherwise specified.

Remove the meat from the freezer, turn on the grinder, and drop the meat one piece at a time into the feed tube.

Let the auger grab each piece of meat and bring it forward toward the blade and through the grinding plate into the chilled bowl. Don't overload the feed tube and start shoving the meat down with the pusher, which will cause the meat to heat up, preventing a clean grind.

The meat should come through the grinder cleanly, in distinct extrusions.

MIXING

STEP 5: To make the farce, begin by measuring out all your add-in ingredients.

If it is looking mushy or smeared, stop the grinder and inspect the blade and die for pieces of tangled sinew. This smearing can also be a sign that your meat has become too warm, in which case you should return it (as well as any meat you've already ground) to the freezer or refrigerator until chilled. Continue grinding until all of the meat has been processed.

STEP 4: Once all of the meat has been ground, drop one or two ice cubes into the grinder feed tube, which will help push out any meat remaining in the feed tube or wrapped around the auger.

In a medium nonreactive bowl, nested in a larger bowl filled with ice, pour the ingredients over the ground meat.

STEP 6: The heat from your hands will warm the mixture slightly, causing the fat to get sticky, and kneading helps release the protein in the meat, which also aids in the emulsification process.

With your hands, mix the spice-water slurry into the meat, using a motion like kneading bread dough, until the spices and meat are well incorporated, about 5 minutes. If you're doing a large batch you can do this step in a mixer, but be conscious of the speed of the mixer and time; you don't want to overmix the farce, which will make it too warm and break the emulsification.

When properly mixed, the meat and fat will be uniformly combined, forming a homogenous paste, and will begin sticking to the bowl.

To check that the meat is properly mixed, spread some on the palm of your hand and turn your hand upside down. If the meat sticks to your palm, it is sufficiently mixed.

At this point you can fold in cheese or other "textured garnish" ingredients such as bacon, nuts, or dried fruit that you want to suspend throughout the sausage.

STEP 7: In a small nonstick frying pan, spread 2 tbsp of the meat mixture into a thin patty using the back of a spoon.

Fry over low heat until cooked through but not browned (because browning changes the flavor profile). If the patty is crumbly and rendering fat, it's a sign that is has not been mixed thoroughly enough.

Slice the patty into strips and squeeze one of the strips between your fingers; some grease may bubble to the surface, but there should not be any foamy bubbles. Foamy bubbles occur when the farce has been overmixed or has become too warm, which damages the cell structure of the meat so that it can no longer absorb the added liquid and fat. There is no fix for a broken farce; you can use it to make meatballs or a pot of chili, but it's not going to make good sausage.

Taste the patty for seasoning and adjust as necessary, frying a second test patty if needed.

You have made sausage! Next, you will stuff the sausage into casings (see page 31) or form it into crepinettes (see page 69).

Press a sheet of parchment paper or plastic wrap directly onto the surface of the meat to help prevent oxidation, cover the bowl tightly with plastic wrap, and refrigerate at least 6 hours or overnight. Even if the farce oxidizes slightly, it won't affect the quality of your finished sausage. (If you have a vacuum-sealer, you can also vacuum-seal the farce.)

Making smooth-textured sausages (see page 112) requires a slightly different method than the Master Technique. Follow the grinding method (steps 1 to 4) as described. Mix the dry ingredients into the meat, but keep the liquid separate. Place the liquid in the freezer until very cold but not frozen.

Working in small batches, transfer the sausage farce to a food processor (keep the remaining meat in the freezer while you work).

If you're using a standard-capacity food processor, each batch should be about 1½ lb/680 g. Add some of the ice water or semi-frozen liquid and process until the farce is smooth.

The longer you can purée the meat while keeping it cool, the smoother and firmer the finished sausage will be. Stop processing when you've reached a smooth but not creamy texture.

Continue adding the cold liquid, which will help keep the farce cool, counteracting the warming effects of the machine and friction.

Constantly monitor the temperature using an infrared thermometer and stop processing before the temperature reaches 40°F/4°C.

If the temperature of the farce does reach 40°F/4°C, transfer the processor bowl to the refrigerator and chill for 15 minutes before resuming. If you overfill the food processor bowl, the farce will overheat and "break," appearing creamy when finished.

If the farce gets too warm it will make a grainy sausage that leaks fat and bubbles when you cook it, so pay close attention to the temperature as you process.

Repeat step 7 from the Master Technique. Repeat with remaining farce and liquid until it has all been processed. Cover the bowl tightly with plastic wrap and refrigerate overnight. If you have a commercial-grade vacuum-sealer, you can vacuum-seal the farce, which will remove air bubbles; vacuum-sealers made for home use don't have the same power, so if that's all you have access to you can skip this step, though your finished sausage will be pocked with small air bubbles. The following day, proceed with stuffing as described in the following steps.

STUFFING

STEP 8: Have your cleaned, soaked casings at the ready (for more information about selecting and preparing casings, see page 13).

Hold the casings in a bowl of ice water or refrigerate until you're ready to begin stuffing.

Untangle the casings and begin to open them to make the stuffing process easier. Hold one end of each piece of casing up to the nozzle of the sink faucet and support it with your other hand. Gently turn on the water and let it run through the casings to rinse them and check for holes. (If there are any holes in the casings, cut out the pieces with the holes.)

STEP 9: Remove the chilled farce and equipment from the refrigerator.

Load the farce into the canister of the sausage stuffer, compressing it very lightly to remove any air bubbles.

Replace the lid. Ready two bowls: one empty, for collecting any burst sausage, and one filled with water, which you can use to lubricate your work surface and stuffer, as well as your sausage pricker. Assemble some clean baking sheets for your finished sausages.

STEP 10: Moisten the nozzle of the sausage stuffer with water, and then load the casings on the nozzle, taking care not to double up the casings.

Gently begin cranking the sausage stuffer; as soon as you see the meat come out of the nose of the stuffer, stop and crank backward to halt the forward movement.

STEP 11: Moisten your work surface with water, which will prevent the sausages from sticking. With one hand, start cranking the sausage stuffer slowly and steadily. Once the farce starts to fill the casing, remove the air by pinching and tying a knot.

Pull 4 to 5 in/10 to 12 cm of casing off the end of the nozzle, but don't knot it.

Your free hand should be on the casing as the sausage is being extruded, helping guide it along.

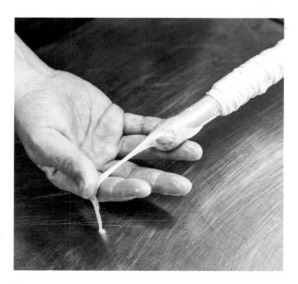

As the sausage is extruded, arrange it on your work surface in a pinwheel.

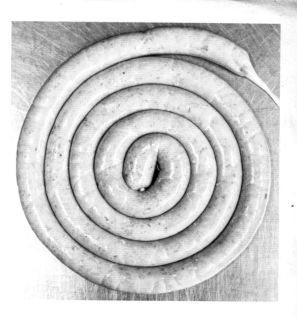

If you see an air pocket, prick the casing with the sausage pricker.

The casings should be full enough so when you twist the sausage into links the farce will be tight in the casing, but not so full that they will burst when twisted.

If the casing splits, simply cut out the damaged bit of casing and discard. Reserve the farce that burst through the casing and add it back into the stuffer.

TWISTING

STEP 12: Gently knot at the end of the sausage rope. Beginning at one end of the sausage rope, measure off a length of sausage.

Pinch the sausage gently to form your first link, and twist forward for about seven rotations.

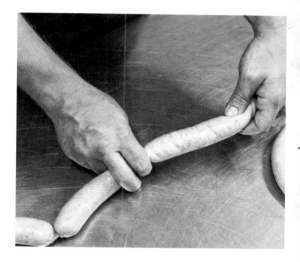

Repeat this process, alternating forward and backward, until you reach the open end of the casing.

Form the second link, and this time, pinch firmly and twist backward.

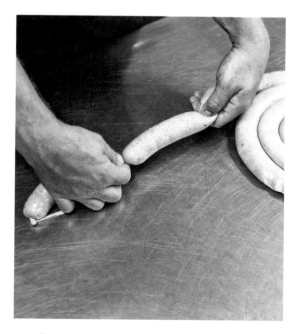

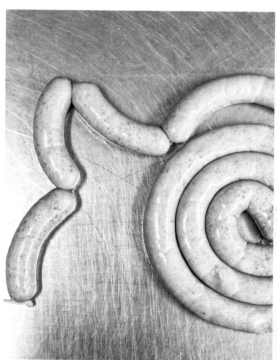

Twist the open end right at the last bit of sausage to seal off the whole coil, and then tie a knot. For larger, heavier sausages that are cased in beef middles or bungs, twist the links as directed, then tie off each link at both ends with a length of kitchen twine.

STEP 13: It's best to let fresh sausage sit or hang overnight, refrigerated, so that the meat adheres to the casing, making for an especially snappy sausage. A sausage that dries overnight will also smoke more evenly and the smoked sausage will have a better color. You can place the sausage on a wire rack set over a rimmed baking sheet or, if possible, hang your fresh sausage in the refrigerator so that it is exposed to air on all sides.

This master technique is utilized, in part or in full, in every recipe in this book.

Cooking and Keeping

You can make the greatest sausage in the world, but if you don't cook it correctly or store it properly you can easily ruin all of your hard work. In essence, sausage cookery should be approached just like you approach all meat cookery: with care.

Regardless of which method you're using, raw sausages should be cooked until they reach the correct internal temperature. Too high a temperature and you risk splitting the casing and drying out the interior; too low and you risk a sausage that has, at best, an unpleasant texture and, at worst, is a health risk. Cooking a sausage is no different than cooking a steak: No matter how you choose to do it—and we give suggestions for the best approach for each of the recipes in the book—you want to cook it to the perfect point of doneness. The following methods will ensure success.

GRILLING

A caramelized sausage hot off the grill is one of life's simple, great pleasures. I prefer using a charcoal grill and hardwood charcoal, which burns hot and clean, without the addition of the chemicals that are used to treat most briquettes.

I use a chimney to start my charcoal.

When the coals are glowing dump them into a kettle grill and add a few more lumps of hardwood charcoal (or some small logs) to the smoldering pile and let the fire cook down for at least 30 minutes, until there is a solid bed of medium-hot coals.

Rushing is a common griller's mistake; take time to get the coals right before you start grilling your sausage.

When the coals are ready, rake one-third of them to one side of the grill to create a multi-zonal fire; the sausages can then be moved from a hot zone to a cool zone as they cook, ensuring they get caramelized and cooked through, but not charred.

Before beginning, lightly oil both the grill grate and the exterior of your sausages with oil, which will help prevent sticking. If the sausages stick and the casings tear, the juices flow out, which can result in a dry sausage. Start the sausages on the grill over the hotter zone.

If you notice a lot of fat dripping from them, it's a sign that the coals are still too hot; if this is the case, move the sausages to the cooler zone of the grill.

Dripping fat results in flare-ups, which in turn cause the exterior of your sausage to burn before the interior has cooked through.

Raw sausages plump up as they cook because cooked protein swells in the casing and the fat liquefies, creating delicious juice. The goal is to gently, slowly cook the sausage so that the casing caramelizes—but doesn't split—in about the same time it takes for the sausage to cook through. Just as with any raw meat on the grill, doneness can be determined by touch and temperature. When the sausage is fully cooked it should be firm to the touch but should not look shriveled; insert a metal cake tester into the center of the sausage and press it to the top of your hand. If it feels hot, the sausage is ready. You can also use an instant thermometer to check the temperature. Don't cut into the sausage to determine doneness, because all of the juices will leak out.

For fully cooked sausages, the goal is to heat them through evenly and brown the exterior, but because they have already been cooked there is no risk of undercooking. Fully cooked sausages are best grilled over medium heat. At that temperature the casings will brown, creating a textural contrast to the meat within, but it's not so hot that the casings will split, releasing the juice. If the sausage has been cooked by smoking, I like to char it a bit more, because I think some char further complements the smoky flavor. If the sausage has been poached, I don't want to overwhelm the delicate flavor of the meat, so I usually opt for a nice golden-brown exterior.

If your grill is equipped with a rotisserie, you can also use it to grill sausages. To do this, you should keep the string of sausage links unbroken, and thread it around the fingers of the rotisserie, spacing them evenly; the sausages will then be suspended over the grill surface.

POACHING

Poaching is an excellent way to cook sausage fully while maintaining its juiciness. It's a method that's well suited to soft sausages, which are too delicate to grill or panfry; I also poach firm and smooth sausages. In general I avoid poaching coarse sausages, because the fat in a coarse sausage melts easily in the hot poaching liquid, rendering out and resulting in a dry sausage.

Poached sausages can be eaten immediately, or they can be chilled fully in an ice bath and refrigerated, then heated through and browned in a pan or on a grill when you're ready to serve them.

Doing this provides a textural contrast, but it also has a practical application: If you're serving a lot of people at a barbecue or event, or in a restaurant setting, you are only warming the sausage through, not cooking it, which saves time and guesswork.

I most commonly poach sausages in plain water or beer with half an onion.

You could certainly use wine or stock or any other liquid, such as apple cider or the liquid leftover from cooking beans; you can also poach the sausage with the beans as they cook.

No matter the poaching liquid you use, the basic method is the same: Insert a probe-style thermometer into the center of one of the raw links. Bring the liquid to a boil in a vessel large enough to accommodate the liquid and sausages without boiling over, then add the raw sausages, including the one with the probe thermometer. When the liquid returns to a bare simmer, cover the pan, remove from the heat, and let stand for 15 minutes or until the sausage reaches the internal temperature specified in the recipe. Beef, lamb, and pork sausages should be poached to an internal temperature of 145°F/63°C. Larger smooth pork sausages that are intended to be served cold, such as bologna and bierwurst, should be poached to an internal temperature of 155°F/68°C, and boudin noir should be poached to an internal temperature of 160°F/71°C.

A probe thermometer is useful because it allows you to know the internal temperature of your sausage without uncovering the pot and losing the accumulated heat and steam. Because the liquid is at its hottest when you add the sausages and gets cooler from that point on, it's virtually impossible to overcook sausages with this method. As a rule of thumb you should have twice as much liquid (by volume) as you do raw sausage; this will ensure that the links cook evenly. Remember about displacement; when you add the raw sausages, the level of the poaching liquid will rise, so choose a pot that's large enough to accommodate the sausages in a single batch, or poach them in multiple batches.

Remove the sausage from the poaching liquid and let stand for 10 minutes. The sausages are then ready to eat, or you can chill them fully in an ice bath, then refrigerate them. When ready to eat, heat on a grill or in a pan until the exterior is browned and the sausage is heated through.

Alternatively, large batches of sausages can also be steam-cooked in a commercial steam oven; set the temperature of the steam for 20°F/11°C above the desired final internal temperature for your sausage and cook until the probe thermometer registers the desired internal temperature. Smaller batches of sausage can be steamed in a lidded bamboo steamer set over a pan of vigorously simmering water. As for the oven method for large batches, steam the links until a probe thermometer inserted in the center registers the temperature specified in the recipe.

SMOKING

Smoking serves two primary purposes: It's a gentle way of cooking a sausage at a low temperature, and it adds another layer of flavor to the finished sausage. Smoked sausages also adhere tightly to the casing, creating that appealing "snappy" texture found in hot dogs and pepperoni.

Because smoke is an assertive flavor, I generally choose to smoke sausages that are boldly seasoned and/or firmly textured. Smoke would overpower the flavors of a more delicate sausage, such as the Chicken-Beer Sausage (page 120), but it is complementary to robustly flavored sausages such as Liverwurst (page 128) and Summer Sausage (page 84).

Electric smokers offer the most control, because you can set the temperature and maintain it throughout the cooking period. You can add smoldering wood chips for flavor without having to build a large enough fire to cook the sausages. These types of smokers have built-in racks; you can place your sausages directly on the racks or suspend them, but in either case you want to be sure not to overcrowd the smoker. The goal is to allow the smoke to circulate easily around the links.

The amount of wood chips or logs that you add to your smoker will determine how smoky your finished sausage is.

This is not a perfect science, so you'll have to do some experimenting to determine how smoky you like your sausages. Because the cooking time must remain the same in order to cook the sausages through, adjustments to the smoke level need to be made by adding fewer or more wood chips. I like to use hickory, apple, cherry, or any other hardwood chips.

I prefer to make the sausages the day before I plan to smoke them. I place them on a cooling rack set over a rimmed baking sheet or hang them, uncovered, in the refrigerator and leave them overnight.

This step gives the casings some time to dry, which will help the smoke cling better to the surface. After I smoke the sausages, I refrigerate them overnight a second time, uncovered, which allows the smoke to mellow and the flavors to meld.

If you do not have a smoker, you can also smoke sausages in your oven. Heat the oven to the desired temperature and suspend the sausages from the oven racks. Place a small pile of wood chips in a large disposable aluminum baking pan and light them on fire (I like to use a blowtorch for this). When the chips are smoldering, transfer the aluminum pan to the oven. Check periodically to ensure that the wood chips are still smoldering or to add more as necessary. If your oven has a convection feature, make sure that it is turned off when you're smoking, otherwise the fan will extinguish the smoldering wood chips.

Regardless of whether you are using an electric smoker or your oven, you should set the temperature to 170°F/77°C and smoke the sausage until doneness is reached, 45 to 60 minutes. Beef, lamb, and pork sausages should be smoked to an internal temperature of 145°F/63°C, poultry sausages to an internal temperature of 160°F/71°C. Insert a probe-style thermometer into one of the links before you add it to the smoker; that way you can monitor the internal temperature without continually opening the smoker, which would lower the temperature and release the smoke.

You should not set the temperature of your smoker or oven above 170°F/77°C. At any higher temperature the fat in the sausage will melt and drip out, both lowering your yield and resulting in a dry final product. Once the sausages have reached the desired internal temperature, they are then fully cooked and can be eaten immediately or cooled and stored and later steamed or gently grilled until heated through.

PANFRYING

One of the simplest ways to prepare sausage is to cook it on a griddle or in a sauté pan. This method is especially well suited to coarse sausages or to sausages that are stuffed in sheep casings, which are more delicate than hog casings and have a greater risk of bursting on the grill. I will also occasionally cook soft sausages using this method.

Heat a pan over medium heat and add a film of oil. When the pan is hot, add the sausages.

Cook the sausages, turning them gently, until they are browned on all sides and cooked within.

Do not cut the sausage in half to check doneness, as you'll release all of the juices. Instead, insert an instant-read thermometer into the center of one link to check. For poultry sausages, the internal temperature should be 155°F/68°C. For beef, lamb, and pork sausages, cook to an internal temperature of 145°F/63°C.

In the case of soft sausages, I often add a few additional tablespoons of butter to the pan and baste the sausages with the hot fat so they cook from all sides; you can also add some sprigs of rosemary or thyme to the hot fat, which add a nice, herbal flavor.

This cooking method is excellent for sausages that have been previously poached or smoked, as it's a slow way of heating them through quickly and gently.

FREEZING

If I can avoid it, I prefer not to freeze sausages. But there are times, for reasons of convenience or necessity, that it makes sense to freeze them. Because the casings are delicate and can tear easily in the freezing and thawing process, I recommend first open-freezing the links (see page 23) on a parchment paper–lined baking sheet. Ensure that the links are not touching, then freeze until firm.

Vacuum-seal the frozen links or transfer them to a resealable plastic freezer bag—it's wise to pack the sausages in the quantities that you will later eat them, so you can pull entire packages from the freezer for thawing.

Thaw the frozen sausages in the refrigerator overnight before you cook them. Do not refreeze thawed sausages, as the quality and texture will suffer. It's very important to label sausages before they go into the freezer with the type, the date the sausages were made, and whether they are fully cooked.

CHAPTER 2

COARSE SAUSAGE

merguez

goat sausage with peppers

chorizo

maple-bacon
breakfast sausage

bacon, cheddar,
and beef links

stinky taleggio
crepinette

Coarse sausage is the most basic type of sausage. It's a family that includes breakfast sausage as well as the Italian-style links you get at the state fair or ballpark. Boldly flavored and juicy, the pieces of fat and meat in this type of sausage remain distinct, giving the sausage a crumbly texture. For this reason, coarse-style sausage farce is often left uncased; it can be browned in a pan or formed into meatballs.

Coarse-style sausages are entry-level sausages, perfect for fledgling sausage-makers. You don't have to be terribly concerned about the amount of fat or liquid in a coarse sausage; well-marbled meat of any kind (about 75 percent lean, 25 percent fat), combined with salt, herbs, and spices, will make a good coarse sausage.

Master Ratio for Coarse Sausage

	U.S. MEASUREMENT	GRAMS	% OF TOTAL (100%)
Lean meat (about 95% lean, 5% fat)	1.80 lb	817	60.00
Not-so-lean meat (about 75% lean, 25% fat)	0.90 lb	409	30.00
Hard fat	⅓ cup	68	5.00
Liquid	¼ cup	48	3.50
Fine sea salt	1 tbsp	20	1.50

BACON, CHEDDAR, AND BEEF LINKS

YIELD: 3 LB/1.4 KG

	U.S. MEASUREMENT	GRAMS	% OF TOTAL (100%)
Boneless lean beef (95% lean, 5% fat), such as round, sirloin, neck, plate, or shank, cut into 1-in/2.5-cm cubes	1.25 lb	571	41.96
Boneless fatty beef (75% lean, 25% fat), such as boneless short rib or brisket	0.60 lb	273	20.49
Bacon, cut into 1-in/2.5-cm pieces	0.60 lb	273	20.49
Ice water	¼ cup	42	3.08
Fine sea salt	1½ tsp	16	1.20
Freshly ground black pepper	2 tbsp	14	1.00
Fresh thyme leaves	2 tbsp	7	0.50
Freshly grated horseradish	2 tbsp	7	0.50
Grated Cheddar cheese	1 cup	147	10.78
Hog casings, rinsed			

Consider this a hamburger in sausage form. We like to serve it on a bun with the traditional burger toppings: shredded lettuce, sliced tomatoes, and our Shhh . . . Sauce, which is 4505 Meats' secret sauce.

1. Place the beef and bacon on a rimmed baking sheet, transfer to the freezer, and chill until crunchy on the exterior but not frozen solid (see page 23).

2. In a small bowl, combine the water, salt, black pepper, thyme, and horseradish and stir to combine.

3. Nest a large mixing bowl in a bowl filled with ice. Grind the meat and bacon through the small die of the grinder into the bowl set in ice (see page 24).

4. Add the spice mixture to the meat and stir with your hands until well incorporated; the mixture will look homogenous and will begin sticking to the bowl (see page 25). Fold the Cheddar cheese into the sausage.

5. Spoon 2 tbsp of the meat mixture into a nonstick frying pan and spread into a thin patty. Cook the test patty over low heat until cooked through but not browned. Taste for seasoning and adjust as necessary.

6. Press a sheet of parchment paper or plastic wrap directly on the surface of the meat to prevent oxidation, then cover the bowl tightly with plastic wrap and refrigerate overnight. Alternatively, you can vacuum-seal the farce.

7. Stuff the sausage into the hog casings (see page 31) and twist into links (see page 36).

8. The sausages can be grilled (see page 38), or the links can be smoked (see page 43) at 170°F/77°C, until the internal temperature of the sausage reaches 145°F/63°C, 45 to 60 minutes. The sausages are then fully cooked, and can be reheated on a grill when you're ready to eat them.

BUTCHER'S SAUSAGE

YIELD: 3 LB/1.4 KG

	U.S. MEASUREMENT	GRAMS	% OF TOTAL (100%)
Lean pork meat (about 95% lean, 5% fat), cut into 1-in/2.5-cm cubes	1.20 lb	524	38.51
Pork heart, cut into small pieces	0.40 lb	175	12.83
Pork liver, cut into small pieces	0.40 lb	175	12.83
White wine	½ cup	113	8.27
Cold water	¼ cup	61	4.46
Finely chopped fresh parsley	2 tbsp	9	0.64
Fine sea salt	2 tbsp	7	0.50
Coarsely ground black pepper	2 tbsp	8	0.57
Red pepper flakes	1 tsp	2	0.13
Finely chopped fresh sage leaves	1 tsp	2	0.13
Fresh thyme leaves	1 tsp	2	0.13
Cooked meat from the pig's head, tongue, or trotters (see facing page), coarsely chopped	0.60 lb	286	21.00
Hog casings, rinsed			

Sausages originated as a way to use up meat scraps, and this British-style butcher's sausage is a perfect example of that. The blend is a lean pork muscle, heart, and liver, with meat from the pig's head, tongue, or trotters adding richness. I like to make this sausage in a smaller size, forming it into links about the length of an average breakfast sausage. Like breakfast sausage, it's great alongside eggs.

1. Place the lean pork, heart, and liver on a rimmed baking sheet; transfer to the freezer; and chill until crunchy on the exterior but not frozen solid (see page 23).

2. In a small bowl, add the wine, water, parsley, salt, black pepper, red pepper flakes, sage, and thyme and stir to combine.

3. Nest a large mixing bowl in a bowl filled with ice. Grind the meat through the small die of the grinder into the bowl set in ice (see page 24).

4. Add the cooked meat and spice mixture to the raw, ground meat and stir with your hands until well incorporated; the mixture will look homogenous and will begin sticking to the bowl (see page 25).

5. Spoon 2 tbsp of the meat mixture into a nonstick frying pan and spread into a thin patty. Cook the test patty over low heat until cooked through but not browned. Taste for seasoning and adjust as necessary.

6. Press a sheet of parchment paper or plastic wrap directly on the surface of the meat to prevent oxidation, then cover the bowl tightly with plastic wrap and refrigerate overnight. Alternatively, you can vacuum-seal the farce.

7. Stuff the sausage into the hog casings (see page 31) and twist into small links (about 4 in/10 cm long) (see page 36).

8. The sausages can be panfried (see page 45) until the internal temperature of the sausage reaches 145°F/63°C.

COOKING PIG'S HEAD, TONGUE, AND TROTTERS

The basic method for preparing pig's head, tongue, and trotters (feet) is the same. Generously salt the cuts and refrigerate overnight. The following day, place the cuts in a pot and cover with cold water by 1 in/2.5 cm. Bring the water to a boil, then pour out the salty water and refill with cold water. Bring the fresh water to a boil and then lower to a simmer. Lightly simmer until the meat pulls easily from the bone but is not falling apart, about 4 hours. Remove the meat from the pot (save the braising liquid), let stand until the meat is cool enough to handle, and then pull the meat and skin off the bone. A cooked pig's head will yield about 3½ lb/1.6 kg meat, feet will yield 4 oz/115 g, and a tongue will yield 4 oz/115 g.

CHORIZO

YIELD: 3 LB/1.4 KG

	U.S. MEASUREMENT	GRAMS	% OF TOTAL (100%)
Boneless pork shoulder (or a combination of cuts, about 75% lean, 25% fat), cut into 1-in/2-cm cubes	1.80 lb	813	59.71
Boiled pork skin (see page 19)	⅓ cup	87	6.30
Beef suet	½ cup	125	9.15
Dried pasilla chiles, stemmed and torn into small pieces	⅓ cup	29	2.15
Dried ancho chiles, stemmed and torn into small pieces	1 tbsp + 1½ tsp	12	0.85
Dried chipotle chile	1	1	0.04
Paprika	1½ tsp	4	0.28
Ground cumin	1½ tsp	4	0.33
Red pepper flakes	½ tsp	1	0.04
Thinly sliced green onions, white and light green parts only	⅔ cup	95	7.00
Ice water	⅓ cup	82	5.99
Tomato paste	2 tbsp	35	2.54
Finely chopped pickled jalapeño chiles (store-bought or homemade, see page 190)	¼ cup	26	1.91
Fine sea salt	1 tbsp + ¾ tsp	27	1.95
Finely chopped fresh cilantro	¼ cup	14	1.00
White vinegar	1½ tsp	6	0.41
Minced garlic	1 tsp	3	0.24
Cure No. 1 (see page 15)	¼ tsp	1	0.11
Hog casings, rinsed			

In addition to the pork meat in this recipe, I also like to include pork skin, which adds collagen to the mix, creating an especially silky sausage. Instead of pork fat, I add beef suet, which has a higher melting point than pork fat. The pieces of suet absorb the seasoning in the sausage, and when you bite into it a capsule of flavor releases in your mouth. When you cook this sausage it generates a lot of flavorful rendered fat. I like to cook vegetables in it to serve alongside the sausage, or save it to drizzle on soup or bread.

1. Place the pork shoulder, pork skin, and beef suet on a rimmed baking sheet; transfer to the freezer; and chill until crunchy on the exterior but not frozen solid (see page 23).

2. In a spice grinder or food processor, combine the dried pasilla, ancho, and chipotle chiles; paprika; ground cumin; and red pepper flakes and process until the chiles are finely ground. Transfer to a medium bowl and stir in the green onions, ice water, tomato paste, pickled jalapeño chiles, salt, cilantro, vinegar, garlic, and Cure No. 1.

3. Nest a large mixing bowl in a bowl filled with ice. Grind the boneless pork, pork skin, and beef suet through the small die of the grinder into the bowl set in ice (see page 24).

4. Add the spice mixture to the meat and stir with your hands until well incorporated; the mixture will look homogenous and will begin sticking to the bowl (see page 25).

5. Spoon 2 tbsp of the meat mixture into a nonstick frying pan and spread into a thin patty. Cook the test patty over low heat until cooked through but not browned. Taste the sausage for seasoning and adjust as necessary.

6. Press a sheet of parchment paper or plastic wrap directly on the surface of the meat to prevent oxidation, then cover the bowl tightly with plastic wrap and refrigerate overnight. Alternatively, you can vacuum-seal the farce.

7. You can leave this sausage uncased, or stuff into sheep casings and twist into links. Cook right away, or freeze them for longer storage (see page 46). The cased sausages can be grilled (see page 38) to an internal temperature of 145°F/63°C; uncased sausage can be crumbled and browned in a sauté pan over medium heat until cooked through.

GOAT SAUSAGE WITH PEPPERS

YIELD: 3 LB/1.4 KG

	U.S. MEASUREMENT	GRAMS	% OF TOTAL (100%)
Boneless goat shoulder and trim, cut into 1-in/2-cm pieces	2.00 lb	914	67.13
Pork back fat, cut into 1-in/2-cm pieces	½ cup	101	7.44
Finely chopped roasted red peppers	⅔ cup	150	10.98
Ice water or cold chicken stock	⅓ cup	78	5.73
Finely chopped Caramelized Onions (page 180)	¼ cup	37	2.74
Finely chopped charred green onions	½ cup	37	2.74
Garlic Confit (page 182)	2½ tsp	8	0.61
Coarsely ground black pepper	2½ tsp	7	0.49
Finely chopped fresh parsley	2½ tsp	7	0.49
Piment d'Espelette	2½ tsp	7	0.49
Finely chopped fresh oregano	1 tbsp	4	0.30
Fine sea salt	1 tsp	12	0.86
Sheep casings, rinsed			

Though goat is not as commonly eaten as other meats, it's delicious, lean, and flavorful and makes an exceptional sausage. I love the flavor of roasted peppers and the fruity heat of French piment d'Espelette. Because it's stuffed into a sheep casing, this sausage is a great choice for people who don't eat pork. This recipe includes charred green onions. You can char them on a gas or charcoal grill until blackened and soft, or cook them in a cast-iron pan.

1. Place the goat and pork fat on a rimmed baking sheet, transfer to the freezer, and chill until crunchy on the exterior but not frozen solid (see page 23).

2. In a medium bowl, add the roasted peppers, ice water, caramelized onions, green onions, garlic confit, black pepper, parsley, piment d'Espelette, oregano, and salt and stir to combine.

3. Nest a large mixing bowl in a bowl filled with ice. Grind the goat and pork fat through the small die of the grinder into the bowl set in ice (see page 24).

4. Add the spice mixture to the meat and stir with your hands until well incorporated; the mixture will look homogenous and will begin sticking to the bowl (see page 25).

5. Spoon 2 tbsp of the meat mixture into a nonstick frying pan and spread into a thin patty. Cook the test patty over low heat until cooked through but not browned. Taste the sausage for seasoning and adjust as necessary.

6. Press a sheet of parchment paper or plastic wrap directly on the surface of the meat to prevent oxidation, then cover the bowl tightly with plastic wrap and refrigerate overnight. Alternatively, you can vacuum-seal the farce.

7. Stuff the sausage into the sheep's casings (see page 31) and twist into small links (about 4 in/10 cm long) (see page 36).

8. Cook the sausages right away, or freeze them for longer storage (see page 46). These sausages are best cooked in a sauté pan or griddle over medium-high heat to an internal temperature of 145°F/63°C. If you want, after the sausages have been cooked and removed from the pan, you can cook vegetables in the accumulated fat. The sausages can also be grilled over indirect heat (see page 38), but beware of the dripping fat, which can produce flare-ups and cause the sausage to become dry.

MAPLE-BACON BREAKFAST SAUSAGE

YIELD: 3 LB/1.4 KG

	U.S. MEASUREMENT	GRAMS	% OF TOTAL (100%)
Boneless pork shoulder (or a combination of cuts, about 75% lean, 25% fat), cut into 1-in/2.5-cm cubes	2.10 lb	981	72.00
Diced bacon	0.50 lb	245	18.00
Finely chopped fresh parsley	2¼ tsp	3	0.22
Ice water	¼ cup	42	2.00
Maple syrup	⅓ cup	84	6.15
Fine sea salt	1½ tsp	11	0.80
Coarsely ground black pepper	½ tsp	1	0.07
Red pepper flakes	1 tsp	2	0.15
Finely chopped fresh sage	2¼ tsp	3	0.22
Finely chopped fresh thyme leaves	2¼ tsp	3	0.22
Finely grated ginger	½ tsp	1	0.07
Ground fenugreek	½ tsp	1	0.04
Ground nutmeg	½ tsp	1	0.06
Sheep casings (optional)			

This is your quintessential morning sausage, perfect alongside pancakes or stacked with a fried egg on a flaky biscuit (see page 196). It just tastes like breakfast: the addition of smoky bacon, real maple syrup, and the classic breakfast sausage flavoring duo, sage and black pepper, all conspire to create the best breakfast sausage ever. Next to our hot dogs, this is probably the most popular sausage we make. It also makes for some killer white sausage gravy, if you're so inclined.

1. Place the pork and bacon on a rimmed baking sheet, transfer to the freezer, and chill until crunchy on the exterior but not frozen solid (see page 23).

2. In a small bowl, add the parsley, ice water, maple syrup, salt, black pepper, red pepper flakes, sage, thyme, ginger, fenugreek, and nutmeg and stir to combine.

3. Nest a large mixing bowl in a bowl filled with ice. Grind the pork and bacon through the small die of the grinder into the bowl set in ice (see page 24).

4. Add the spice mixture to the meat and stir with your hands until well incorporated; the mixture will look homogenous and will begin sticking to the bowl (see page 25).

5. Spoon 2 tbsp of the meat mixture into a nonstick frying pan and spread into a thin patty. Cook the test patty over low heat until cooked through but not browned. Taste the sausage for seasoning and adjust as necessary.

6. Press a sheet of parchment paper or plastic wrap directly on the surface of the meat to prevent oxidation, then cover the bowl tightly with plastic wrap and refrigerate overnight. Alternatively, you can vacuum-seal the farce.

7. This sausage can be left uncased, either loose or formed into patties, or stuffed into sheep casings (see page 31) and twisted into links (see page 36).

8. Breakfast sausages (both patties and links) are best cooked to an internal temperature of 145°F/63°C, either in a sauté pan or on a griddle over medium heat until browned.

MERGUEZ

	U.S. MEASUREMENT	GRAMS	% OF TOTAL (100%)
Boneless lamb neck or boneless lamb shoulder, cut into 1-in/2.5-cm pieces	2.40 lb	1,101	80.82
Ice water	½ cup	122	8.99
Harissa spice mix (store-bought or homemade, see page 184)	1 cup	62	4.55
Finely diced red onion	2 tbsp	20	1.44
Thinly sliced green onions, white and light green parts only	⅓ cup	16	1.21
Tomato paste	1 tbsp	13	0.99
Finely chopped fresh cilantro	¼ cup	12	0.90
Finely chopped pickled jalapeños (store-bought or homemade, see page 190)	1 tbsp	9	0.67
Minced garlic	1½ tsp	4	0.26
Finely chopped fresh oregano	1 tsp	2	0.17
Sheep casings, rinsed			

This flavorful North African–style lamb sausage is probably one of my favorites. I like to make it with lamb neck, which comprises a few small muscles surrounded by hard fat. The fat is incredibly flavorful and absorbs the seasonings in the sausage instead of melting the way pork fat does. If you can't find lamb neck at your local butcher shop, boneless lamb shoulder can be substituted.

You can use my recipe for harissa or substitute a store-bought harissa dry spice blend. If all you're able to find is harissa paste, you should use the same amount but omit the tomato paste in this recipe.

1. Place the lamb on a rimmed baking sheet, transfer to the freezer, and chill until crunchy on the exterior but not frozen solid (see page 23).

2. In a medium bowl, add the ice water, harissa, red onion, green onions, tomato paste, cilantro, pickled jalapeños, garlic, and oregano and stir to combine.

3. Nest a large mixing bowl in a bowl filled with ice. Grind the meat through the small die of the grinder into the bowl set in ice (see page 24).

4. Add the spice mixture to the meat and stir with your hands until well incorporated; the mixture will look homogenous and will begin sticking to the bowl (see page 25).

5. Spoon 2 tbsp of the meat mixture into a nonstick frying pan and spread into a thin patty. Cook the test patty over low heat until cooked through but not browned. Taste the sausage for seasoning and adjust as necessary.

6. Press a sheet of parchment paper or plastic wrap directly on the surface of the meat to prevent oxidation, then cover the bowl tightly with plastic wrap and refrigerate overnight. Alternatively, you can vacuum-seal the farce.

7. Stuff the sausage into the sheep casings (see page 31) and twist into links (see page 36).

8. Cook the sausages right away or freeze them for longer storage (see page 46). Merguez are best cooked in a sauté pan or griddle over medium-high heat to an internal temperature of 145°F/63°C (see page 45). They can also be grilled over indirect heat (see page 38), but beware of the dripping fat, which can produce flare-ups and cause the sausage to become dry. If you want, after the sausages have been cooked and removed from the pan, you can cook vegetables in the accumulated fat to serve alongside.

SPICY ITALIAN SAUSAGE

....

YIELD: 3 LB/1.4 KG

	U.S. MEASUREMENT	GRAMS	% OF TOTAL (100%)
Boneless pork shoulder (or a combination of cuts, about 75% lean, 25% fat), cut into 1-in/2.5-cm cubes	2.80 lb	1,286	94.40
Ice water	2 tbsp	20	1.50
White wine	2 tbsp	20	1.50
Fine sea salt	1½ tsp	16	1.20
Fennel seeds	1½ tsp	15	1.10
Red pepper flakes	1½ tsp	4	0.30
Hog casings, rinsed (optional)			

This is a straightforward recipe for a classic sausage, with some heat from the red pepper flakes and a good amount of fennel seeds, which are left whole. My idea of sausage heaven is an Italian on a soft bun, piled high with cooked peppers and onions. If you want, you can leave this sausage uncased, rolling it into meatballs or using it as a pizza topping.

1. Place the pork on a rimmed baking sheet, transfer to the freezer, and chill until crunchy on the exterior but not frozen solid (see page 23).

2. In a medium bowl, add the ice water, wine, salt, fennel seeds, and red pepper flakes and stir to combine.

3. Nest a large mixing bowl in a bowl filled with ice. Grind the pork shoulder through the small die of the grinder into the bowl set in ice (see page 24).

4. Add the spice mixture to the meat and stir with your hands until well incorporated; the mixture will look homogenous and will begin sticking to the bowl (see page 25).

5. Spoon 2 tbsp of the meat mixture into a nonstick frying pan and spread into a thin patty. Cook the test patty over low heat until cooked through but not browned. Taste the sausage for seasoning and adjust as necessary.

6. Press a sheet of parchment paper or plastic wrap directly on the surface of the meat to prevent oxidation, then cover the bowl tightly with plastic wrap and refrigerate overnight. Alternatively, you can vacuum-seal the farce.

7. You can leave this sausage uncased, or stuff into hog casings (see page 31) and twist into links (see page 36). Cook right away or freeze for longer storage (see page 46). The cased sausages can be grilled (see page 38) to an internal temperature of 145°F/63°C; uncased sausage can be crumbled and browned in a sauté pan over medium heat, or added raw to a pizza before it's baked.

STINKY TALEGGIO CREPINETTE

YIELD: 3 LB/1.4 KG

	U.S. MEASUREMENT	GRAMS	% OF TOTAL (100%)
Boneless pork shoulder (or a combination of cuts, about 75% lean, 25% fat), cut into 1-in/2.5-cm cubes	2.00 lb	1,083	79.50
Water	2 tbsp	19	1.42
Sauternes	2 tbsp	19	1.42
Fine sea salt	1½ tsp	14	1.04
Fines herbes	⅓ cup	28	2.09
Coarsely ground black pepper	1 tsp	5	0.35
Taleggio cheese, cut into slices	1 cup	193	14.18
Caul fat, soaked (see page 13)			

This is a simple pork sausage with the special addition of Taleggio cheese. Taleggio is a pungent, washed-rind cow's milk cheese from Italy. It's creamy and rich, with a funky flavor. To make the cheese easier to slice, freeze it briefly and lightly oil the blade of your knife before cutting.

1. Place the pork on a rimmed baking sheet, transfer to the freezer, and chill until crunchy on the exterior but not frozen solid (see page 23).

2. In a medium bowl, add the water, Sauternes, salt, fines herbes, and black pepper and stir to combine.

3. Nest a large mixing bowl in a bowl filled with ice. Grind the meat through the small die of the grinder into the bowl set in ice (see page 24).

4. Add the herb mixture to the meat and stir with your hands until well incorporated; the mixture will look homogenous and will begin sticking to the bowl (see page 25).

5. Spoon 2 tbsp of the meat mixture into a nonstick frying pan and spread into a thin patty. Cook the test patty over low heat until cooked through but not browned. Taste the sausage for seasoning and adjust as necessary.

6. Press a sheet of parchment paper or plastic wrap directly on the surface of the meat to prevent oxidation, then cover the bowl tightly with plastic wrap and refrigerate overnight. Alternatively, you can vacuum-seal the farce.

7. Form the meat mixture into 4-oz/115-g patties, about ½ in/12 mm thick, and place on a rimmed baking sheet. Position the caul fat on your work surface and, with a sharp knife, cut the caul into 12-in-/30.5-cm-diameter circles. Place the taleggio in the center of the farce. Wrap each patty in caul fat. The crepinettes are best grilled over indirect heat (see page 38) or cooked in an oiled pan over medium heat (see page 45); start the crepinettes seam-side down, turning once midway through cooking, until an instant-read thermometer inserted in the center registers 145°F/63°C.

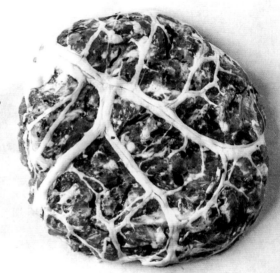

RABBIT CREPINETTE

YIELD: 3 LB/1.4 KG

	U.S. MEASUREMENT	GRAMS	% OF TOTAL (100%)
Boneless rabbit, cut into 1-in/2.5-cm cubes	1.00 lb	469	34.42
Rabbit liver and heart	0.20 lb	101	7.40
Pork shoulder (or a combination of cuts, about 75% lean, 25% fat), cut into 1-in/2.5-cm cubes	1.00 lb	469	34.42
Boiled pork skin (see page 19)	0.20 lb	94	6.90
Green olives, such as Picholine or Lucques, pitted and finely chopped	½ cup	70	5.16
Ice water	2 tbsp	26	1.89
Finely chopped green onions, both green and white parts	½ cup	26	1.89
Finely diced red onion	2 tbsp	23	1.73
Finely diced fennel bulb	2 tbsp	23	1.73
White wine	2 tbsp	20	1.44
Spicy brown mustard	2 tsp	10	0.72
Finely chopped fresh parsley	¼ cup	14	1.02
Fine sea salt	1½ tsp	14	1.02
Coarsely ground black pepper	1½ tsp	4	0.26
Caul fat, soaked (see page 13)			

A crepinette is a small, disk-shaped sausage that is wrapped in caul fat instead of stuffed into a casing. These rabbit "meat pillows" are some of my favorites; green olives and mustard complement the mild meat. I like to include the rabbit liver and heart, but if you don't have access to those cuts, you can just increase the amount of rabbit meat in the recipe.

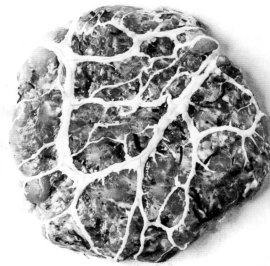

1. Place the rabbit, rabbit liver and heart, pork shoulder, and pork skin on a rimmed baking sheet; transfer to the freezer; and chill until crunchy on the exterior but not frozen solid (see page 23).

2. In a medium bowl add the olives, ice water, green onions, red onion, fennel, wine, mustard, parsley, salt, and black pepper and stir to combine.

3. Nest a large mixing bowl in a bowl filled with ice. Grind the meat through the small die of the grinder into the bowl set in ice (see page 24).

4. Add the spice mixture to the meat and stir with your hands until well incorporated; the mixture will look homogenous and will begin sticking to the bowl (see page 25).

5. Spoon 2 tbsp of the meat mixture into a nonstick frying pan and spread into a thin patty. Cook the test patty over low heat until cooked through but not browned. Taste the sausage for seasoning and adjust as necessary.

6. Press a sheet of parchment paper or plastic wrap directly on the surface of the meat to prevent oxidation, then cover the bowl tightly with plastic wrap and refrigerate overnight. Alternatively, you can vacuum-seal the farce.

7. Form the meat mixture into 4-oz/115-g patties, about ½ in/12 mm thick, and place on a rimmed baking sheet. Position the caul fat on your work surface and, with a sharp knife, cut the caul into 12-in-/30.5-cm-in-diameter circles. Wrap each patty in caul fat. The crepinettes are best grilled over indirect heat (see page 38) or cooked in an oiled pan over medium heat (see page 45); start the crepinettes seam-side down, turning once midway through cooking, until an instant-read thermometer inserted in the center registers 145°F/63°C.

CHAPTER 3

FIRM
SAUSAGE

lao sausage

venison and juniper sausage

linguiça

↑ beer bratwurst

jerk doggy ↗

smoked polish
sausage

The sausages in this chapter are tight, solid links, such as kielbasa and summer sausage, that contain little water in comparison to the amount of protein. This ratio is almost the reverse of that in soft sausages, and they typically contain very little other than meat, which accounts for the texture.

Because of the texture, these types of sausage take well to smoking, and because the fat is well incorporated into the meat, very little fat pools out from a cooked firm sausage, which is one of the things that distinguishes a firm sausage from a coarse one. In addition, a firm sausage holds its shape when sliced (think pepperoni), rather than crumbling (think Italian sausage). They typically contain no vegetables or fillers, so they hold their shape well. A firm sausage doesn't always require a casing, either, as the farce can be formed around a metal or bamboo skewer and grilled, or formed into a patty and wrapped in caul fat to create a crepinette (see page 67).

Master Ratio for Firm Sausage

	U.S. MEASUREMENT	GRAMS	% OF TOTAL (100%)
Lean meat (about 75% lean, 25% fat)	1.90 lb	858	63.00
Extra-lean meat (about 95% lean, 5% fat)	0.80 lb	381	28.00
Fatty meat (such as bacon or pork belly)	⅓ cup	61	4.50
Ice water	2 tbsp	40	2.90
Fine sea salt	2¼ tsp	22	1.60

BEER BRATWURST

YIELD: 3 LB/1.4 KG

	U.S. MEASUREMENT	GRAMS	% OF TOTAL (100%)
Boneless pork shoulder (or a combination of pork cuts, about 75% lean, 25% fat), cut into 1-in/2.5-cm cubes	1.90 lb	844	62.02
Boneless veal shoulder or breast, cut into 1-in/2.5-cm cubes	0.80 lb	362	26.61
Pale ale	½ cup	121	8.87
Fine sea salt	1 tbsp	22	1.60
Sugar	1 tsp	4	0.31
Caraway seeds	1 tsp	2	0.18
Dry mustard powder	½ tsp	1	0.10
Fresh thyme leaves	1 tsp	1	0.09
Ground ginger	½ tsp	1	0.08
Freshly grated nutmeg	¼ tsp	0.46	0.03
Cure No. 1 (see page 15)	¼ tsp	1	0.11
Hog casings, rinsed			

When I was a kid growing up in the Midwest, my friends and I would always pick up big packages of bratwurst to grill while watching sporting events. I wanted to re-create the sausage of my youth, and I think these bratwurst come pretty close. This is a simple, classic sausage; serve it on a crunchy roll with mustard and sauerkraut.

1. Place the pork and veal on a rimmed baking sheet, transfer to the freezer, and chill until crunchy on the exterior but not frozen solid (see page 23).

2. Pour the ale into a shallow baking dish, transfer to the freezer, and chill until the ale is semi-frozen.

3. In a small bowl, add the salt, sugar, caraway seeds, mustard powder, thyme, ginger, nutmeg, and Cure No. 1 and stir to combine.

4. Nest a large mixing bowl in a bowl filled with ice. Grind the meat through the small die of the grinder into the bowl set in ice (see page 24).

5. Add the spice mixture to the meat and stir with your hands until well incorporated; the mixture will look homogenous and will begin sticking to the bowl (see page 25).

6. Spoon 2 tbsp of the meat mixture into a nonstick frying pan and spread into a thin patty. Cook the test patty over low heat until cooked through but not browned. Taste the sausage for seasoning and adjust as necessary.

7. Press a sheet of parchment paper or plastic wrap directly on the surface of the meat to prevent oxidation, then cover the bowl tightly with plastic wrap and refrigerate overnight. Alternatively, you can vacuum-seal the farce.

8. Stuff the sausage into the hog casings (see page 31) and twist into links (see page 36).

9. Poach the links (see page 41) in water or lager-style beer until an instant-read thermometer inserted into the center of the sausage registers 145°F/63°C. The poached sausages can be grilled (see page 38) and then eaten immediately, or chilled fully in an ice bath and refrigerated, or frozen for longer storage (see page 46). When you're ready to eat them, grill again or cook in a pan over medium heat until browned and heated through (see page 45).

JERK DOGGY

YIELD: 3 LB/1.4 KG

	U.S. MEASUREMENT	GRAMS	% OF TOTAL (100%)
Boneless pork shoulder (or a combination of cuts, about 75% lean, 25% fat), cut into 1-in/2.5-cm cubes	1.60 lb	748	54.95
Boneless beef round or sirloin (or a combination of cuts, about 95% lean, 5% fat), cut into 1-in/2.5-cm cubes	0.80 lb	371	27.23
Finely chopped fresh parsley	½ cup	35	2.60
Finely chopped fresh cilantro	½ cup	35	2.60
Jalapeños, stemmed and finely chopped	¼ cup	30	2.21
Finely chopped fresh basil	½ cup	28	2.08
Fine sea salt	1 tbsp	25	1.82
Brown sugar	2 tbsp	20	1.45
Thinly sliced green onions, both green and white parts	⅓ cup	17	1.22
Finely chopped pineapple	1½ tbsp	14	1.04
Coarsely ground black pepper	1½ tsp	8	0.62
Dried ancho chile, stemmed, torn into small pieces, and pulsed in a spice grinder until finely ground	1 tbsp	7	0.52
Ice water	1½ tsp	7	0.52
Finely chopped yellow onion	1½ tsp	5	0.36
Habañero chile powder	1 tsp	3	0.21
White vinegar	1 tsp	2	0.18
Ground nutmeg	½ tsp	1	0.10
Sheep casings, rinsed			

This recipe is loosely based on a jerk shrimp recipe I used to make at a restaurant I worked at early in my career; I slather a similar spice paste on roasted pigs. It gets its spiciness from three different varieties of chile (jalapeño, habañero, and ancho), balanced by the sweetness of brown sugar and pineapple. The fresh herbs give it a brightness of flavor that's often missing in jerk.

1. Place the pork and beef on a rimmed baking sheet, transfer to the freezer, and chill until crunchy on the exterior but not frozen solid (see page 23).

2. In a medium bowl, add the parsley, cilantro, jalapeños, basil, salt, brown sugar, green onions, pineapple, black pepper, ancho chile, ice water, yellow onion, habañero chile powder, vinegar, and nutmeg and stir to combine.

3. Nest a large mixing bowl in a bowl filled with ice. Grind the meat through the small die of the grinder into the bowl set in ice (see page 24).

4. Add the spice mixture to the meat and stir with your hands until well incorporated; the mixture will look homogenous and will begin sticking to the bowl (see page 25).

5. Spoon 2 tbsp of the meat mixture into a nonstick frying pan and spread into a thin patty. Cook the test patty over low heat until cooked through but not browned. Taste the sausage for seasoning and adjust as necessary.

6. Press a sheet of parchment paper or plastic wrap directly on the surface of the meat to prevent oxidation, then cover the bowl tightly with plastic wrap and refrigerate overnight. Alternatively, you can vacuum-seal the farce.

7. Stuff the sausage into the sheep casings (see page 31) and twist into links (see page 36).

8. Eat the sausages right away, or freeze them for longer storage (see page 46). Jerk dogs are best cooked in a sauté pan or griddle over medium-high heat to an internal temperature of 145°F/63°C (see page 45). If you want, after the sausages have been cooked and removed from the pan, you can cook vegetables in the accumulated fat. They can also be grilled over indirect heat (see page 38), but beware of the dripping fat, which can result in flare-ups and cause the sausage to become dry.

LAO SAUSAGE

YIELD: 3 LB/1.4 KG

	U.S. MEASUREMENT	GRAMS	% OF TOTAL (100%)
Boneless pork shoulder (or a combination of cuts, about 75% lean, 25% fat), cut into 1-in/2.5-cm cubes	1.80 lb	846	62.12
Boneless lean pork, such as loin or leg (about 95% lean, 5% fat), cut into 1-in/2.5-cm cubes	0.80 lb	376	27.61
Diced bacon	⅓ cup	60	4.43
Fine sea salt	2¼ tsp	19	1.41
Ice water	1 tbsp + ¾ tsp	15	1.09
Finely chopped fresh mint	1½ tsp	6	0.43
Finely chopped fresh basil	1½ tsp	6	0.43
Minced lemongrass	1½ tsp	6	0.43
Finely chopped fresh cilantro	1½ tsp	6	0.43
Peeled and minced galangal	1½ tsp	4	0.33
Minced shallot	1½ tsp	4	0.33
Minced garlic	1½ tsp	4	0.33
Minced Thai chile	¾ tsp	4	0.33
Fish sauce	1 tsp	2	0.17
Minced kaffir lime leaves	¾ tsp	2	0.13
Hog casings, rinsed			

This pork sausage is flavored with some quintessentially Southeast Asian ingredients, including lemongrass, galangal, kaffir lime, and fish sauce. Lemongrass is woody and fibrous, so peel away the outer leaves of the stalk and trim to a length of 3 in/7.5 cm, then mince. At the market in the summertime, we grill uncased patties of this sausage and serve it with a watermelon-basil-mint salad alongside.

1. Place both porks and the bacon on a rimmed baking sheet, transfer to the freezer, and chill until crunchy on the exterior but not frozen solid (see page 23).

2. In a medium bowl, add the salt, ice water, mint, basil, lemongrass, cilantro, galangal, shallot, garlic, Thai chile, fish sauce, and lime leaves and stir to combine.

3. Nest a large mixing bowl in a bowl filled with ice. Grind the pork and bacon through the small die of the grinder into the bowl set in ice (see page 24).

4. Add the spice mixture to the meat and stir with your hands until well incorporated; the mixture will look homogenous and will begin sticking to the bowl (see page 25).

5. Spoon 2 tbsp of the meat mixture into a nonstick frying pan and spread into a thin patty. Cook the test patty over low heat until cooked through but not browned. Taste the sausage for seasoning and adjust as necessary.

6. Press a sheet of parchment paper or plastic wrap directly on the surface of the meat to prevent oxidation, then cover the bowl tightly with plastic wrap and refrigerate overnight. Alternatively, you can vacuum-seal the farce.

7. Stuff the sausage into hog casings (see page 31) and twist into links (see page 36).

8. Smoke the links (see page 43) until an instant-read thermometer inserted into the center of the sausage registers 145°F/63°C. The smoked sausages can be eaten immediately, or chill them fully in an ice bath and refrigerate, or freeze them for longer storage (see page 46). When you're ready to eat them, grill the links over indirect heat (see page 38) or cook in a pan over medium heat until browned and heated through (see page 45).

LINGUIÇA

YIELD: 3 LB/1.4 KG

	U.S. MEASUREMENT	GRAMS	% OF TOTAL (100%)
Boneless pork shoulder (or a combination of pork cuts, about 75% lean, 25% fat), cut into 1-in/2.5-cm cubes	1.60 lb	716	52.60
Diced bacon	0.75 lb	341	25.07
Boiled pork skin (see page 19)	⅓ cup	68	5.00
Port wine	1½ tbsp	20	1.50
Cure No. 1 (see page 15)	½ tsp	3	0.22
Cold water	½ cup	123	9.00
Fine sea salt	2¼ tsp	18	1.30
Red wine vinegar	1½ tsp	7	0.50
Granulated garlic	½ tsp	1	0.07
Finely chopped fresh oregano	¾ tsp	1	0.07
Nonfat dry milk powder	½ cup	41	3.02
Paprika	2 tbsp	10	0.72
Cayenne pepper	1 tbsp	7	0.50
Sugar	1 tbsp	6	0.43
Hog casings, rinsed			

This is one of the first sausages we grilled and sold at the market. We serve it topped with peppers and onions, a classic combination that always makes me think of baseball games, but it's often served with shellfish, especially in Portuguese communities. We have one regular customer, Harris, who asks for this sausage every week. Sour, sweet, and smoky—this one's for you, Harris.

1. Place the pork shoulder, bacon, and pork skin on a rimmed baking sheet; transfer to the freezer; and chill until crunchy on the exterior but not frozen solid (see page 23).

2. In a small bowl, add the port, Cure No. 1, water, salt, vinegar, granulated garlic, oregano, milk powder, paprika, cayenne, and sugar and stir to combine.

3. Nest a large mixing bowl in a bowl filled with ice. Grind the pork, bacon, and skin through the small die of the grinder into the bowl set in ice (see page 24).

4. Add the spice mixture to the meat and stir with your hands until well incorporated; the mixture will look homogenous and will begin sticking to the bowl (see page 25).

5. Spoon 2 tbsp of the meat mixture into a nonstick frying pan and spread into a thin patty. Cook the test patty over low heat until cooked through but not browned. Taste the sausage for seasoning and adjust as necessary.

6. Press a sheet of parchment paper or plastic wrap directly on the surface of the meat to prevent oxidation, then cover the bowl tightly with plastic wrap and refrigerate overnight. Alternatively, you can vacuum-seal the farce.

7. Stuff the sausage into the hog casings (see page 31) and twist into links (see page 36).

8. Smoke the links (see page 43) at 170°F/77°C, until the internal temperature of the sausage reaches 145°F/63°C, 45 to 60 minutes. Remove the sausages from the smoker, let cool slightly, then transfer to the refrigerator and let stand, uncovered, overnight. The linguiça are then fully cooked, and can be finished on a grill or in a pan.

SMOKED POLISH SAUSAGE

YIELD: 3 LB/1.4 KG

	U.S. MEASUREMENT	GRAMS	% OF TOTAL (100%)
Boneless pork shoulder (or a combination of cuts, about 75% lean, 25% fat), cut into 1-in/2.5-cm cubes	2.25 lb	902	66.25
Pork back fat, cut into 1-in/2.5-cm cubes	1 cup	286	21.00
Ice water	½ cup	97	7.15
Fine sea salt	2¼ tsp	18	1.29
Minced garlic	1½ tsp	5	0.36
Coarsely ground black pepper	1½ tsp	4	0.29
Sugar	½ tsp	2.5	0.18
Finely chopped fresh oregano	1 tsp	1.5	0.11
Nonfat dry milk powder	⅓ cup	43	3.15
Cure No. 1 (see page 15)	½ tsp	3	0.22
Hog casings, rinsed			

There are hundreds of different varieties of Polish sausage, and this is my version. When I was young, my grandfather, who we all call Papa, used to go to Wisconsin for work and he'd always return with hanks of kielbasa and lengths of summer sausage; this smoked link pays homage to those special deliveries. I like to slather this sausage with Beer Mustard (page 174).

1. Place the pork shoulder and back fat on a rimmed baking sheet, transfer to the freezer, and chill until crunchy on the exterior but not frozen solid (see page 23).

2. In a small bowl, add the ice water, salt, garlic, black pepper, sugar, oregano, milk powder, and Cure No. 1 and stir to combine.

3. Nest a large mixing bowl in a bowl filled with ice. Grind the meat and fat through the large die of the grinder into the bowl set in ice (see page 24).

4. Add the spice mixture to the meat and stir with your hands until well incorporated; the mixture will look homogenous and will begin sticking to the bowl (see page 25).

5. Spoon 2 tbsp of the meat mixture into a nonstick frying pan and spread into a thin patty. Cook the test patty over low heat until cooked through but not browned. Taste the sausage for seasoning and adjust as necessary.

6. Press a sheet of parchment paper or plastic wrap directly on the surface of the meat to prevent oxidation, then cover the bowl tightly with plastic wrap and refrigerate overnight. Alternatively, you can vacuum-seal the farce.

7. Stuff the sausage into the hog casings (see page 31) and twist into links (see page 36).

8. Smoke the links (see page 43) at 170°F/77°C, until the internal temperature of the sausage reaches 145°F/63°C, 45 to 60 minutes. Remove the sausages from the smoker, let cool, then transfer to the refrigerator and let stand, uncovered, overnight. When you're ready to eat them, they can be steamed (see page 42) or gently grilled (see page 38) until heated through.

SUMMER SAUSAGE

YIELD: 3 LB/1.4 KG

	U.S. MEASUREMENT	GRAMS	% OF TOTAL (100%)
Boneless lean beef (95% lean, 5% fat), such as sirloin, neck, plate, or shank, cut into 1-in/2.5-cm cubes	1.70 lb	766	56.22
Boneless pork shoulder (or a combination of pork cuts, about 75% lean, 25% fat), cut into 1-in/2.5-cm cubes	0.85 lb	388	28.51
Boiled pork skin (see page 19)	¼ cup	57	4.20
Diced bacon	¼ cup	57	4.21
Ice water	2 tbsp	24	1.77
Fine sea salt	1 tbsp	23	1.68
Dextrose or sugar	1½ tsp	15	1.10
Paprika	2 tbsp	10	0.73
Cure No. 1 (see page 15)	1 tsp	6	0.44
Coarsely ground black pepper	1 tsp	5	0.39
Granulated garlic	1 tsp	5	0.37
Red pepper flakes	¾ tsp	3	0.19
Onion powder	¾ tsp	3	0.19
Beef middles, rinsed			

When I was growing up, I used to accompany my grandfather on road trips. Whenever I dragged my heels about going, he'd promise me a McDonald's egg-and-sausage biscuit sandwich. On one trip, we spent the night in the back of Grandpa's truck and instead of the promised Egg McMuffin, Grandpa pulled out some day-old biscuits, a hard-boiled egg, and a length of summer sausage and proceeded to make my biscuit sandwich. I'd been had.

I prefer to use dextrose in place of sugar because the sausage hangs for a week before it is smoked, during which time the dextrose raises the pH, giving the finished sausage its tangy flavor.

1. Place the beef, pork shoulder, pork skin, and bacon on a rimmed baking sheet; transfer to the freezer; and chill until crunchy on the exterior but not frozen solid (see page 23).

2. In a small bowl, add the ice water, salt, dextrose, paprika, Cure No. 1, black pepper, granulated garlic, red pepper flakes, and onion powder and stir to combine.

3. Nest a large mixing bowl in a bowl filled with ice. Grind the meat, pork skin, and bacon through the small die of the grinder into the bowl set in ice (see page 24).

4. Add the spice mixture to the meat and stir with your hands until well incorporated; the mixture will look homogenous and will begin sticking to the bowl (see page 25).

5. Spoon 2 tbsp of the meat mixture into a nonstick frying pan and spread into a thin patty. Cook the test patty over low heat until cooked through but not browned. Taste the sausage for seasoning and adjust as necessary.

6. Press a sheet of parchment paper or plastic wrap directly on the surface of the meat to prevent oxidation, then cover the bowl tightly with plastic wrap and refrigerate overnight. Alternatively, you can vacuum-seal the farce.

7. Stuff the sausage into the beef middles (see page 31), twist into links, then tie off each link with kitchen twine (see page 36). Let the sausage hang, refrigerated, for seven days before smoking.

8. Smoke the links (see page 43) at 170°F/77°C, until the internal temperature of the sausage reaches 145°F/63°C, 45 to 60 minutes. Remove from the smoker and let cool, then transfer to the refrigerator and let stand, uncovered, overnight. When you're ready to eat them, chill and slice or gently grill (see page 38) until heated through.

TURKEY, APPLE, AND CAMPARI SAUSAGE

YIELD: 3 LB/1.4 KG

	U.S. MEASUREMENT	GRAMS	% OF TOTAL (100%)
Boneless, skin-on turkey breast, cut into 1-in/2.5-cm cubes	1.40 lb	621	45.59
Boneless pork shoulder (or a combination of cuts, about 75% lean, 25% fat)	0.90 lb	433	31.81
Pork back fat, cut into 1-in/2.5-cm cubes	½ cup	101	7.42
Apple, cut into ¼-in/6-mm cubes	½ cup	76	5.60
Apple cider	2 tbsp	40	2.97
Honey	2 tbsp	29	2.12
Campari	2 tbsp	21	1.55
Fine sea salt	2¼ tsp	17	1.23
Finely chopped fresh peppercress or watercress	¼ cup	12	0.85
Thinly sliced green onions, both green and white parts	2 tbsp	7	0.53
Coarsely ground black pepper	1½ tsp	3	0.21
Fresh thyme leaves	1½ tsp	2	0.12
Hog casings, rinsed			

Not surprisingly, I first started making this sausage around Thanksgiving, when we had some surplus turkey meat left over from making our annual batch of turduckens. Campari, an herbaceous Italian aperitif, adds a touch of bitterness, countered by cubes of sweet apple. You can use any firm apple for this recipe. While you're grilling the sausages, double-down on the Campari by drinking a Negroni.

1. Place the turkey, pork shoulder, and pork fat on a rimmed baking sheet; transfer to the freezer; and chill until crunchy on the exterior but not frozen solid (see page 23).

2. In a medium bowl, add the apple cubes, apple cider, honey, Campari, salt, peppercress, green onions, black pepper, and thyme and stir to combine.

3. Nest a large mixing bowl in a bowl filled with ice. Grind the turkey, pork, and pork fat through the small die of the grinder into the bowl set in ice (see page 24).

4. Add the apple mixture to the meat and stir with your hands until well incorporated; the mixture will look homogenous and will begin sticking to the bowl (see page 25).

5. Spoon 2 tbsp of the meat mixture into a nonstick frying pan and spread into a thin patty. Cook the test patty over low heat until cooked through but not browned. Taste the sausage for seasoning and adjust as necessary.

6. Press a sheet of parchment paper or plastic wrap directly on the surface of the meat to prevent oxidation, then cover the bowl tightly with plastic wrap and refrigerate overnight. Alternatively, you can vacuum-seal the farce.

7. Stuff the sausage into the hog casings (see page 31) and twist into links (see page 36).

8. Poach the links (see page 41) until an instant-read thermometer inserted into the center of the sausage registers 155°F/68°C. The poached sausages can be eaten immediately, or chill fully in an ice bath and refrigerate for up to 2 days (any longer than that and the apple in the sausage starts to break down), or freeze them for longer storage (see page 46). When you're ready to eat them, grill over indirect heat (see page 38) or cook in a pan over medium heat (see page 45) until browned and heated through.

VENISON AND JUNIPER SAUSAGE

YIELD: 3 LB/1.4 KG

	U.S. MEASUREMENT	GRAMS	% OF TOTAL (100%)
Boneless venison shoulder, cut into 1-in/2.5-cm cubes	1.80 lb	844	62.00
Guanciale (cured pork jowl) or pancetta, diced	0.60 lb	268	19.70
Diced beef suet	½ cup	136	9.95
Gin	2 tbsp	29	2.15
Ice water	2 tbsp	29	2.15
Fine sea salt	1 tbsp	20	1.45
Finely chopped fresh parsley	¼ cup	12	0.90
Finely chopped fresh sage	¼ cup	12	0.90
Coarsely ground black pepper	1 tbsp	8	0.60
Juniper berries, finely ground	3 tsp	3	0.20
Sheep casings, rinsed			

Venison has great flavor but is very lean, so this sausage benefits from the addition of both beef suet and *guanciale* (cured pork jowl). The juniper and gin give the sausage a deep, woodsy flavor, which seems a fitting match for venison. If you can't find guanciale, substitute pancetta.

1. Place the venison, guanciale, and suet on a rimmed baking sheet; transfer to the freezer; and chill until crunchy on the exterior but not frozen solid (see page 23).

2. In a small bowl, add the gin, ice water, salt, parsley, sage, black pepper, and juniper berries and stir to combine.

3. Nest a large mixing bowl in a bowl filled with ice. Grind the venison, guanciale, and suet through the small die of the grinder into the bowl set in ice (see page 24).

4. Add the herb mixture to the meat and stir with your hands until well incorporated; the mixture will look homogenous and will begin sticking to the bowl (see page 25).

5. Spoon 2 tbsp of the meat mixture into a nonstick frying pan and spread into a thin patty. Cook the test patty over low heat until cooked through but not browned. Taste the sausage for seasoning and adjust as necessary.

6. Press a sheet of parchment paper or plastic wrap directly on the surface of the meat to prevent oxidation, then cover the bowl tightly with plastic wrap and refrigerate overnight. Alternatively, you can vacuum-seal the farce.

7. Stuff the sausage into the sheep casings (see page 31) and twist into links (see page 36).

8. These sausages are best grilled over indirect heat (see page 38) or panfried over medium heat (see page 45) until they reach an internal temperature of 145°F/63°C. The sausages may also be frozen (see page 46).

CHAPTER 4
SOFT SAUSAGE

boudin noir with
winter fruit

duck cotechino

the kermit

cajun boudin

scrapple

scottish white
pudding

guinea hen and
kimchee links

Like the smooth sausages described in chapter 1, soft-textured sausages contain a higher percentage of liquid and fat as compared to the coarse or firm-textured sausages described in chapters 2 and 3. But unlike smooth sausages, which require the additional technical step of whipping the sausage farce in a food processor, soft sausages are lightly mixed, not puréed. The challenge to making soft sausages is that you're trying to push the ratio, adding as much liquid and fat as possible.

It's this additional liquid and larger percentage of fat that give soft sausages their custardy texture and richness. Because the farce is so delicate, soft sausages in this chapter are typically poached, rather than smoked or grilled.

Master Ratio for Soft Sausage

	U.S. MEASUREMENT	GRAMS	% OF TOTAL (100%)
Lean meat (about 75% lean, 25% fat)	2.20 lb	9,801	72.00
Fat	½ cup	133	9.80
Ice-cold liquid	½ cup	136	10.00
Extra-lean meat (about 95% lean, 25% fat)	⅓ cup	95	7.00
Fine sea salt	1½ tsp	5	1.20

BOUDIN NOIR WITH WINTER FRUIT

··

YIELD: 3 LB/1.4 KG

	U.S. MEASUREMENT	GRAMS	% OF TOTAL (100%)
Boneless pork shoulder (or a combination of cuts, about 75% lean, 25% fat), cut into 1-in/2.5-cm cubes	1.10 lb	449	36.60
Pig's blood	0.90 lb	393	28.83
Eggs	3	136	10.00
Heavy cream	2 tbsp	37	2.70
Fine sea salt	1 tbsp	30	2.23
Sugar	¾ tsp	9	0.68
Cure No. 1 (see page 15)	¼ tsp	1	0.11
Breadcrumbs	1 cup	67	4.93
Finely chopped radicchio	⅔ cup	14	1.00

	U.S. MEASUREMENT	GRAMS	% OF TOTAL (100%)
Ground nutmeg	1½ tsp	5	0.35
Ground anise	1½ tsp	5	0.35
Ground cinnamon	¼ tsp	1	0.05
Coarsely ground black pepper	1½ tsp	4	0.32
Ground cloves	¼ tsp	1	0.02
Nonfat dry milk powder	⅓ cup	51	3.74
Red pepper flakes	¼ tsp	1	0.03
Ground ginger	¼ tsp	1	0.06
Finely diced fresh pear, apple, or fuyu persimmon	⅔ cup	109	8.00
Hog casings, rinsed			

CONTINUED

I think of boudin noir as a cased custard. In addition to the pork and blood, the delicate sausage also contains eggs and cream, which gives it a creamy texture. I add breadcrumbs as a binder in place of rice or flour, which you'll find in some versions, because I think it gives the sausage the best flavor.

I like to make and serve this richly spiced sausage in the winter, when I have access to nice winter fruit. It's a 4505 Meats holiday favorite, and during the long days that precede the holiday our crew eats boudin noir and eggs for breakfast before we start the workday.

1. Place the pork on a rimmed baking sheet, transfer to the freezer, and chill until crunchy on the exterior but not frozen solid (see page 23).

2. Pour the blood into a shallow baking dish, transfer to the freezer, and chill until very cold but not frozen.

3. In a medium bowl, add the eggs, cream, salt, sugar, Cure No. 1, breadcrumbs, radicchio, nutmeg, anise, cinnamon, black pepper, cloves, milk powder, red pepper flakes, and ginger and stir to combine.

4. Nest a large mixing bowl in a bowl filled with ice. Grind the meat through the small die of the grinder into the bowl set in ice (see page 24).

5. Transfer the meat to the bowl of a mixer fitted with the paddle attachment. Add the spice mixture to the meat and mix on medium speed until the mixture is sticky. Reduce the mixer speed to low and slowly add the blood. Continue mixing on low until it is well incorporated; it should look homogenous and will stick to the bowl. Gently fold in the fruit.

6. Spoon a few tablespoons of the mixture onto a length of plastic wrap. Fold the plastic wrap over the sausage to tightly encase it, then twist the two ends to form a link.

7. Bring a small saucepan of water to a boil over high heat, then gently drop the plastic-wrapped link into the water, return the water to a simmer, then remove the pan from the heat, cover, and let stand 15 minutes. Unwrap the link, taste for seasoning, and adjust as necessary.

8. Press a sheet of parchment paper or plastic wrap directly on the surface of the meat to prevent oxidation, then cover the bowl tightly with plastic wrap and refrigerate overnight. Alternatively, you can vacuum-seal the farce.

9. Stuff the sausage into the hog casings (see page 31) and twist into links (see page 36).

10. Poach the links (see page 41) until an instant-read thermometer inserted into the center of the sausage registers 160°F/71°C. The poached sausages can be eaten immediately, or chill fully in an ice bath. The poached sausages can be vacuum-sealed or transferred to a plastic storage bag and refrigerated, or you can freeze them for longer storage (see page 46). When you're ready to eat them, grill over indirect heat (see page 38) or cook in butter in a pan over medium heat (see page 45) until browned and heated through, basting frequently with the butter. If you'd like, you can add additional fruit to the pan and cook it alongside the sausage until softened.

CAJUN BOUDIN

YIELD: 3 LB/1.4 KG

	U.S. MEASUREMENT	GRAMS	% OF TOTAL (100%)
Boneless pork shoulder (or a combination of cuts, about 75% lean, 25% fat), cut into 1-in/2.5-cm cubes	1.20 lb	535	39.28
Pork liver, cut into 1-in/2.5-cm pieces	0.30 lb	147	10.80
Reserved pork cooking liquid	¼ cup	67	4.91
Cooked white rice, at room temperature	2 cups	468	34.37
Finely chopped fresh parsley	¼ cup	15	1.13
Minced green bell pepper	¼ cup	33	2.46
Finely chopped green onions, both green and white parts	¼ cup	12	0.88
Fine sea salt	1½ tsp	13	0.98
Freshly ground black pepper	½ tsp	1	0.09
Fresh thyme leaves	¾ tsp	1	0.09
Cayenne pepper	½ tsp	1	0.09
Boiled pork skin (see page 19)	⅔ cup	67	4.92
Hog casings, rinsed			

Unlike every other sausage in this book, the ingredients for the Cajun Boudin are fully cooked before the farce is mixed and stuffed. This sausage has roots in Louisiana, and traditionally contains both pork liver and rice. It's usually formed into links, but can also be formed into balls, rolled in breadcrumbs, and fried; boudin balls are a popular gas-station snack throughout Cajun country.

1. Place the pork shoulder in a medium saucepan and cover with 1 in/ 2.5 cm of water. Bring to a boil over high heat, then reduce the heat so the liquid is barely simmering and cook, replenishing the water as necessary, until the pork shoulder is tender, about 1½ hours. Add the liver and cook 15 minutes longer. Drain, reserving ¼ cup/60 ml of the pork cooking liquid. Let the meat cool until you can handle it.

2. In a medium bowl, add the reserved pork cooking liquid, rice, parsley, bell pepper, green onions, salt, black pepper, thyme, and cayenne and stir to combine.

3. Nest a large mixing bowl in a bowl filled with ice. Grind the cooked pork shoulder, liver, and pork skin through the small die of the grinder into the bowl set in ice (see page 24).

4. Add the rice mixture to the meat and stir with your hands until well incorporated; the mixture will look homogenous and will begin sticking to the bowl (see page 25).

5. Spoon 2 tbsp of the meat mixture into a nonstick frying pan and spread into a thin patty. Cook the test patty over low heat until cooked through but not browned. Taste the sausage for seasoning and adjust as necessary.

6. Press a sheet of parchment paper or plastic wrap directly on the surface of the meat to prevent oxidation, then cover the bowl tightly with plastic wrap and refrigerate overnight. Alternatively, you can vacuum-seal the farce.

7. Stuff the sausage into the hog casings (see page 31) and twist into links (see page 36).

8. The meat in the sausage is fully cooked, but the links must still be smoked (see page 43) for 15 minutes to cook the casings. The smoked sausages can be eaten immediately, or chill them fully in an ice bath and refrigerate, or freeze for longer storage (see page 46). When you're ready to eat them, lightly grill or sear the sausages until heated through or grill over indirect heat (see page 38) until browned and heated through.

DUCK COTECHINO

YIELD: 3 LB/1.4 KG

	U.S. MEASUREMENT	GRAMS	% OF TOTAL (100%)
Boneless pork shoulder (or a combination of cuts, about 75% lean, 25% fat), cut into 1-in/2.5-cm cubes	1.20 lb	526	38.60
Boiled pork skin (see page 19)	0.40 lb	192	14.07
Boneless, skin-on duck thigh, cut into 1-in/2.5-cm cubes	0.75 lb	342	25.12
Ice water	⅓ cup	80	5.86
Pickled red onion (see page 191, variation)	⅓ cup	55	4.02
Finely diced fennel bulb	¼ cup	41	3.02
Finely chopped green onions, dark green parts only	¼ cup	38	2.81
Finely diced red onion	¼ cup	27	2.01
White wine	2 tbsp	23	1.66
Fine sea salt	1½ tsp	16	1.16
Spicy brown mustard	1 tbsp	11	0.82
Finely minced garlic	1½ tsp	5	0.36
Finely chopped fresh rosemary	1 tbsp	4	0.27
Sugar	½ tsp	2	0.17
Coarsely ground black pepper	½ tsp	1	0.05
Beef middles or hog casings, rinsed			

Cotechino is often paired with lentils and eaten on New Year's Day because it's a dish that's said to bring luck. Traditional versions are made with pork and raw pork skin stuffed into hog casings. Slowly simmered with lentils or white beans, the casing and the pork skin in the sausage soften, releasing collagen, which makes the lentils or beans particularly silky and flavorful. Our not-so-traditional version was created to use up surplus duck that we had on hand after we made our annual batch of turduckens. We stuff the sausage into beef middles and use boiled pork skin, and those two changes mean the cotechino doesn't need to be slowly simmered before eating. It's a streamlined version that doesn't sacrifice flavor.

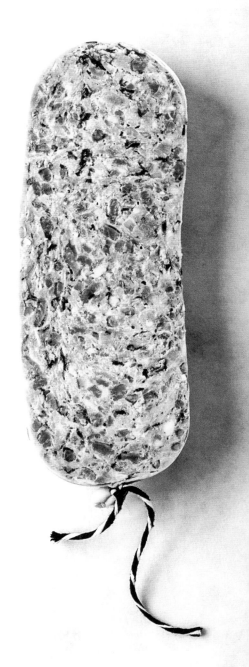

1. Place the pork shoulder, pork skin, and duck thigh on a rimmed baking sheet, transfer to the freezer, and chill until crunchy on the exterior but not frozen solid (see page 23).

2. In a medium bowl, add the ice water, pickled red onion, fennel, green onions, red onion, wine, salt, mustard, garlic, rosemary, sugar, and black pepper and stir to combine.

3. Nest a large mixing bowl in a bowl filled with ice. Grind the pork shoulder, pork skin, and duck meat and skin through the small die of the grinder into the bowl set in ice (see page 24).

4. Add the onion mixture to the meat and stir with your hands until well incorporated; the mixture will look homogenous and will begin sticking to the bowl (see page 25).

5. Spoon 2 tbsp of the meat mixture into a nonstick frying pan and spread into a thin patty. Cook the test patty over low heat until cooked through but not browned. Taste the sausage for seasoning and adjust as necessary.

6. Press a sheet of parchment paper or plastic wrap directly on the surface of the meat to prevent oxidation, then cover the bowl tightly with plastic wrap and refrigerate overnight. Alternatively, you can vacuum-seal the farce.

7. Stuff the sausage into the beef middles (see page 31) and twist into links (see page 36). Tie links with kitchen string every 5 in/12.5 cm to 6 in/15 cm.

8. Poach the links (see page 41) until an instant-read thermometer inserted into the center of the sausage registers 145°F/63°C. The poached sausages can be eaten immediately, or chill them fully in an ice bath and refrigerate, or freeze for longer storage (see page 46). When you're ready to eat the sausages, cut them into medallions and grill or cook in butter in a pan until browned and heated through, basting frequently. Alternatively, warm them in a pot of cooked beans or lentils.

GUINEA HEN AND KIMCHEE LINKS

YIELD: 3 LB/1.4 KG

	U.S. MEASUREMENT	GRAMS	% OF TOTAL (100%)
Boneless, skin-on guinea hen (a 50:50 mixture of light and dark meat), cut into 1-in/2.5-cm cubes	1.10 lb	499	36.81
Boneless pork shoulder (or a mixture of cuts, about 75% lean, 25% fat), cut into 1-in/2.5-cm cubes	0.70 lb	321	23.57
Roughly chopped kimchee	1⅓ cups	214	15.71
Kimchee juice or water	⅓ cup	83	6.13
Finely diced red onion	⅔ cup	118	8.63
Chicharrones (pork rinds), crumbled	1¼ cups	71	5.24
Thinly sliced green onions, white and light green parts only	¼ cup	26	1.92
Minced garlic	1 tbsp	14	1.05
Fine sea salt	1½ tsp	13	0.94
Hog casings, rinsed			

4505 Meats has a stand at the weekly Ferry Plaza Farmers Market in San Francisco, where we sell our killer cheeseburger and sausages. In a neighboring stall are our friends the Lee brothers, owners of Namu restaurant, and their market manager Jeff Kim. Namu serves modern Korean food, and this sausage is inspired by them; we use their kimchee (and its liquid) to make this sausage. If you can't find guinea hen, you can substitute duck or even chicken, but be sure to include the skin, which gives the finished sausage a silky texture. We add our own *chicharrones* to the mix, for a textural contrast.

1. Place the guinea hen meat and skin and the pork shoulder on a rimmed baking sheet, transfer to the freezer, and chill until crunchy on the exterior but not frozen solid (see page 23).

2. In a small bowl, add the kimchee, kimchee juice, red onion, chicharrones, green onions, garlic, and salt and stir to combine.

3. Nest a large mixing bowl in a bowl filled with ice. Grind the guinea hen meat and skin and pork shoulder through the small die of the grinder into the bowl set in ice (see page 24).

4. Add the onion mixture to the meat and stir with your hands until well incorporated; the mixture will look homogenous and will begin sticking to the bowl (see page 25).

5. Spoon 2 tbsp of the meat mixture into a nonstick frying pan and spread into a thin patty. Cook the test patty over low heat until cooked through but not browned. Taste the sausage for seasoning and adjust as necessary.

6. Press a sheet of parchment paper or plastic wrap directly on the surface of the meat to prevent oxidation, then cover the bowl tightly with plastic wrap and refrigerate overnight. Alternatively, you can vacuum-seal the farce.

7. Stuff the sausage into the hog casings (see page 31) and twist into links (see page 36).

8. Poach the links (see page 41) until an instant-read thermometer inserted into the center of the sausage registers 155°F/68°C. The poached sausages can be eaten immediately, or chill them fully in an ice bath and refrigerate, or freeze for longer storage (see page 46). When you're ready to eat the sausages, grill (see page 38) or cook in a pan (see page 45) until browned and heated through.

THE KERMIT

YIELD: 3 LB/1.4 KG

	U.S. MEASUREMENT	GRAMS	% OF TOTAL (100%)
Boneless, skinless frog legs, finely chopped	0.90 lb	416	30.55
Boneless, skin-on chicken thighs, cut into 1-in/2.5-cm cubes	1.50 lb	693	50.90
Pork leaf lard, cut into 1-in/2.5-cm cubes	0.30 lb	139	10.18
Ice water	2 tbsp	20	1.48
White wine	2 tbsp	30	2.22
Finely chopped fresh parsley	⅓ cup	16	1.18
Fine sea salt	1½ tsp	15	1.12
Minced garlic	2 tbsp	14	1.04
Roasted garlic powder	1 tbsp	7	0.51
Coarsely ground black pepper	1 tsp	2	0.15
Lemon juice	¾ tsp	4	0.31
Lemon zest	1½ tsp	2	0.16
Ground coriander	1½ tsp	3	0.20
Sheep casings, rinsed			

Frog's legs have fallen out of fashion in most restaurants, which is a shame. This sausage pays homage to the classic preparation, with lots of lemon, garlic, and fresh parsley. Because frog meat has a softer texture, I use it in combination with chicken thighs to give the sausage more structure. Both of those meats are relatively lean, so I add pork leaf lard, which is the fat surrounding the kidneys, to ensure the sausage is juicy.

1. Place the frog legs, chicken thighs, and pork leaf lard on a rimmed baking sheet, transfer to the freezer, and chill until crunchy on the exterior but not frozen solid (see page 23).

2. In a medium bowl, add the ice water, wine, parsley, salt, garlic, garlic powder, black pepper, lemon juice, lemon zest, and coriander and stir to combine.

3. Nest a large mixing bowl in a bowl filled with ice. Grind the chicken thighs and pork leaf lard through the small die of the grinder into the bowl set in ice (see page 24) and add the frog meat.

4. Add the spice mixture to the meat and stir with your hands until well incorporated; the mixture will look homogenous and will begin sticking to the bowl (see page 25).

5. Spoon 2 tbsp of the meat mixture into a nonstick frying pan and spread into a thin patty. Cook the test patty over low heat until cooked through but not browned. Taste the sausage for seasoning and adjust as necessary.

6. Press a sheet of parchment paper or plastic wrap directly on the surface of the meat to prevent oxidation, then cover the bowl tightly with plastic wrap and refrigerate overnight. Alternatively, you can vacuum-seal the farce.

7. Stuff the sausage into sheep casings (see page 31) and twist into links (see page 36).

8. Poach the links (see page 41) until an instant-read thermometer inserted into the center of the sausage registers 155°F/68°C. The poached sausages can be eaten immediately, or chill them fully in an ice bath and refrigerate, or freeze for longer storage (see page 38). When you're ready to eat the sausages, cook in a pan or griddle (see page 45) until browned and heated through.

SCRAPPLE

YIELD: 3 LB/1.4 KG

	U.S. MEASUREMENT	GRAMS	% OF TOTAL (100%)
Pig liver and/or heart	⅓ cup	69	5.10
Cooked meat from the pig's head, trotters, and tongue (see page 55), coarsely chopped	0.60 lb	279	20.50
Braising liquid from cooking head, trotters, and tongue	1.60 lb	695	51.00
Maple syrup	¼ cup	75	5.50
Cornmeal	1 cup	97	7.10
Corn flour or all-purpose flour	1 cup	97	7.10
Fine sea salt	1 tbsp	23	1.70
Minced garlic	2¼ tsp	10	0.70
Finely ground black pepper	2¼ tsp	5	0.40
Finely chopped fresh sage	1 tbsp	5	0.40
Finely ground coriander	1 tsp	3	0.20
Fresh thyme leaves	2¼ tsp	4	0.30

Pennsylvania Dutch country is where this rustic recipe originated, and where it's still popular today. It's traditionally made with the scraps left over after a pig was butchered into prime cuts, and is an excellent way to make something truly delicious out of very little. The cornmeal-meat mixture sets up into a firm loaf; sliced, panfried in butter, and served alongside eggs, it makes a hearty breakfast.

1. Place the pig liver and/or heart and the cooked meat on a rimmed baking sheet, transfer to the freezer, and chill until crunchy on the exterior but not frozen solid (see page 23).

2. Nest a large mixing bowl in a bowl filled with ice. Grind the pig liver and/or heart and cooked meat through the small die of the grinder into the bowl set in ice (see page 24). Transfer the bowl containing the ground meat to the refrigerator.

3. In a large saucepan over medium-high heat, bring the braising liquid to a vigorous simmer and add the maple syrup. Gradually add in the cornmeal and corn flour, whisking constantly to prevent lumps from forming, then whisk in the salt, garlic, black pepper, sage, coriander, and thyme. Reduce the heat to medium-low and cook the porridge, stirring occasionally with a wooden spoon, until the cornmeal is tender and the mixture resembles cooked polenta, about 45 minutes. Add the ground meat mixture and continue cooking 15 minutes longer.

4. While the cornmeal mixture cooks, lightly grease a 9-by-5-by-3-in/23-by-12-by-7.5-cm loaf pan or terrine mold. Pour the cooked cornmeal-meat mixture into the loaf pan, smoothing the top. Press a piece of plastic wrap on the surface, pressing gently. Let cool to room temperature, then transfer to the refrigerator and let chill overnight.

5. When you are ready to serve the scrapple, slice into ½-in/12-mm slices and fry in butter in a nonstick or cast-iron frying pan, turning once, until deeply browned on both sides.

SCOTTISH WHITE PUDDING

YIELD: 3 LB/1.4 KG

	U.S. MEASUREMENT	GRAMS	% OF TOTAL (100%)
Rolled oats	0.70 lb	330	24.21
Room temperature water	1⅔ cups	377	27.65
Beef suet, cut into 1-in/2.5-cm cubes	0.40 lb	188	13.82
Rendered pork fat	0.10 lb	65	4.75
Milk	⅔ cup	178	13.05
Finely chopped leeks, white and light green parts only	1 cup	129	9.50
Finely chopped leek tops	¼ cup	32	2.37
Fine sea salt	1 tbsp	27	1.97
Flour	2 tbsp	13	0.99
Coarsely ground black pepper	2 tbsp	16	1.18
Ground coriander	1 tbsp	7	0.51
Hog casings, rinsed			

This is a fine example of making something really delicious out of ordinary ingredients. Oats, fortified by beef and pork fat and mixed until creamy, form the basis of this humble sausage. It can be stuffed into hog casings, but you can also pack the sausage into a loaf pan and chill it overnight. The following day, slice the loaf, fry the slices in butter until golden brown, and serve alongside eggs for a stick-to-your-ribs breakfast.

1. Put the oats and water in a large bowl. Stir to combine, then let stand for 30 minutes.

2. In a medium saucepan over medium-low heat, combine the beef suet, two-thirds of the rendered pork fat, and the milk and cook, stirring occasionally, until the fat has melted. Set aside.

3. In a medium sauté pan, heat the remaining pork fat over medium heat. Add the leeks and cook, stirring occasionally, until softened but not browned, about 7 minutes. Transfer to the bowl containing the oats and add the fat-milk mixture, leek tops, salt, flour, black pepper, and coriander and stir to combine. Transfer to the bowl of an electric mixer and mix on low speed until the mixture is homogenous and is sticking to the bowl (see page 25).

4. Spoon 2 tbsp of the meat mixture into a nonstick frying pan and spread into a thin patty. Cook the test patty over low heat until cooked through but not browned. Taste the sausage for seasoning and adjust as necessary.

5. While still warm, stuff the sausage into the hog casings (see page 31) and twist into small (3-in/7.5-cm) links (see page 36).

6. Poach the links (see page 41) until an instant-read thermometer inserted into the center of the sausage registers 145°F/63°C. The poached sausages can be eaten immediately, or chill them fully in an ice bath and refrigerate, or freeze for longer storage (see page 46). When you're ready to eat the sausages, cut them into medallions and lightly sear in a pan until browned and heated through.

CHAPTER 5

SMOOTH SAUSAGE

liverwurst

bierwurst

smoked trout and pork sausage

blood bologna

all-beef hot dogs

foie gras
boudin blanc

Of all the sausages in this book, smooth-textured sausages are the most technically difficult. Though the basic grinding process remains the same, smooth sausages contain a higher percentage of liquid than other sausage types, and require an additional, technical step: the sausage farce must be puréed in a food processor until smooth and creamy, during which time it must remain very cold. The additional air that is incorporated during this step gives the links a fluffy texture, a nice counterpoint to the snappy casing.

Emulsifying agents, like eggs and dry milk powder, are often added to smooth sausage. Adding these emulsifiers makes it possible to incorporate more liquid and, in turn, more fat to the meat. Lean beef is also often added to smooth-textured sausage in combination with other meats. Because beef is a stable protein source with a higher water content than other meats, adding beef can often eliminate the need for other emulsifiers.

Temperature is extremely important when making smooth sausage. Your farce must not ever get warmer than 40°F/4°C or the emulsification will break, just as when making a mayonnaise, and you'll end up with a sausage that has a grainy texture and a greasy mouthfeel. Your meat should be almost frozen before it is ground and you should carefully monitor the temperature when you process the meat, adding crushed ice in place of water to help keep the mixture cool.

Master Ratio for Smooth Sausage

	U.S. MEASUREMENT	GRAMS	% OF TOTAL (100%)
Lean meat (about 95% lean, 5% fat)	2.00 lb	908	66.70
Crushed ice	1¼ cups	272	20.00
Fatty meat, such as bacon or pork belly	0.33 lb	150	11.00
Fine sea salt	1 tbsp	31	2.30

ALL-BEEF HOT DOGS

....

YIELD: 3 LB/1.4 KG

	U.S. MEASUREMENT	GRAMS	% OF TOTAL (100%)
Boneless lean beef (95% lean, 5% fat), such as neck, plate, or shank, cut into 1-in/2.5-cm cubes	2.10 lb	949	69.70
Beef fat, cut into 1-in/2.5-cm cubes	¾ cup	137	10.05
Fine sea salt	2 tbsp	23	1.66
Paprika	1 tsp	10	0.70
Granulated garlic	½ tsp	5	0.40
Coarsely ground black pepper	¼ tsp	4	0.28
Onion powder	¼ tsp	3	0.22
Cure No. 1 (see page 15)	¼ tsp	1	0.11
Crushed ice	1 cup	230	16.88
Sheep casings, rinsed			

When I think of all-beef hot dogs, I think of the small, snappy links served at Gray's Papaya in New York City. They're rich and juicy, griddled until crispy on the outside: the perfect all-beef dog. If you can't find neck, plate, or shank meat, substitute chuck for all of the meat and fat called for in the recipe.

1. Place the meat and fat on a rimmed baking sheet, transfer to the freezer, and chill until crunchy on the exterior but not frozen solid (see page 23).

2. In a small bowl, add the salt, paprika, granulated garlic, black pepper, onion powder, and Cure No. 1 and stir to combine.

3. Nest a large mixing bowl in a bowl filled with ice. Grind the meat and fat through the small die of the grinder into the bowl set in ice (see page 24).

4. Add the spice mixture to the meat and stir with your hands until well incorporated; the mixture will look homogenous and will begin sticking to the bowl (see page 25).

5. Transfer the meat to the bowl of a food processor, add half the crushed ice and process until all of the ice has dissolved, 1 to 2 minutes. Add the remaining crushed ice and continue processing until the mixture is completely smooth, 4 to 5 minutes more. Note: The temperature of your meat during this mixing step is critically important. Its temperature should never rise about 40°F/4°C; work efficiently during this step of the process.

6. Spoon 2 tbsp of the meat mixture into a nonstick frying pan and spread into a thin patty. Cook the test patty over low heat until cooked through but not browned. Taste the sausage for seasoning and adjust as necessary.

7. Press a sheet of parchment paper or plastic wrap directly on the surface of the meat to prevent oxidation, then cover the bowl tightly with plastic wrap and refrigerate overnight. Alternatively, you can vacuum-seal the farce.

8. Stuff the sausage into the sheep casings (see page 31) and twist into links (see page 36).

9. Smoke the links (see page 43) at 170°F/77°C, until the internal temperature of the sausage reaches 145°F/63°C, 45 to 60 minutes. Remove the sausages from the smoker, let cool slightly, then transfer to the refrigerator and let stand, uncovered, overnight. The hot dogs are then fully cooked, and can be finished on a grill (see page 38) or steamed (see page 42).

BIERWURST

YIELD: ONE 3-LB/1.4-KG LOG

	U.S. MEASUREMENT	GRAMS	% OF TOTAL (100%)
Pork back fat, cut into ½-in/12-mm cubes	⅔ cup	139	10.24
Boneless lean beef, such as round, sirloin, neck, plate, or shank (about 95% lean, 5% fat) cut into 1-in/2.5-cm cubes	1.40 lb	614	45.09
Boneless pork shoulder (or a combination of cuts, about 75% lean, 25% fat)	0.60 lb	266	19.52
Diced bacon	⅔ cup	111	8.20
Fine sea salt	1 tbsp	24	1.79
Mustard powder	2¼ tsp	6	0.46
Coarsely ground black pepper	1½ tsp	4	0.30
Fresh thyme leaves	1½ tsp	2	0.15
Coarsely ground coriander	½ tsp	1	0.09
Cure No. 1 (see page 15)	½ tsp	3	0.22
Pale ale	⅔ cup	190	13.94
Beef bung, rinsed			

This is my version of the bologna I grew up eating. It's a three-day process. When it's done, slice it thinly, pile it on a crusty roll, and top with mustard and kraut for a killer sandwich.

1. Place the pork back fat in a medium saucepan and cover with water by ½ in/12 mm. Bring to a boil over high heat and boil for 10 minutes. Drain and transfer the fat cubes to a plate and refrigerate until cold.

2. Place the beef, pork shoulder, and bacon on a rimmed baking sheet, transfer to the freezer, and chill until crunchy on the exterior but not frozen solid (see page 23).

3. In a small bowl, add the salt, mustard powder, black pepper, thyme, coriander, and Cure No. 1 and stir to combine.

4. Nest a large mixing bowl in a bowl filled with ice. Grind the beef, pork shoulder, and bacon through the small die of the grinder into the bowl set in ice (see page 24).

5. Add the spice mixture to the meat and stir with your hands until well incorporated; the mixture will look homogenous and will begin sticking to the bowl (see page 25).

6. Press a sheet of parchment paper or plastic wrap directly on the surface of the meat to prevent oxidation, then cover the bowl tightly with plastic wrap and refrigerate overnight. Alternatively, you can vacuum-seal the farce.

7. Pour the ale into a shallow baking dish, transfer to the freezer, and chill until the ale is semi-frozen, about 40 minutes.

8. Transfer the meat to the bowl of a food processor, add half of the semi-frozen ale and process for 1 to 2 minutes. Add the remaining ale and continue processing until smooth, 4 to 5 minutes longer. Note: The temperature of your meat during this mixing step is critically important. Its temperature should never rise about 40°F/4°C; work efficiently during this step of the process. Depending on the size of your food processor, you may need to do this step in batches. Fold in the chilled backfat.

9. Spoon 2 tbsp of the meat mixture into a nonstick frying pan and spread into a thin patty. Cook the test patty over low heat until cooked through but not browned. Taste the sausage for seasoning and adjust as necessary.

10. Stuff the meat into the beef bung (see page 31); the bierwurst should be about 5 in/12 cm in diameter and 10 in/25 cm long. Let hang, refrigerated, overnight.

11. Smoke the bung (see page 43) at 170°F/77°C, until the internal temperature reaches 145°F/63°C, 45 to 60 minutes. Remove from the smoker, let cool slightly, then transfer to a refrigerator and let stand, uncovered, overnight. When you're ready to eat the sausages, slice thinly with a sharp knife.

BLOOD BOLOGNA

YIELD: ONE 3-LB/1.4-KG LOG

	U.S. MEASUREMENT	GRAMS	% OF TOTAL (100%)
Boneless pork shoulder (or a combination of cuts, about 75% lean, 25% fat), cut into 1-in/2.5-cm cubes	1.90 lb	844	54.00
Diced bacon	⅓ cup	95	6.10
Nonfat dry milk powder	⅓ cup	68	4.35
Fine sea salt	1 tbsp + ¾ tsp	31	2.00
Mustard powder	2¼ tsp	5	0.34
Coarsely ground black pepper	1½ tsp	3	0.17
Ground coriander	½ tsp	1	0.09
Cure No. 1 (see page 15)	½ tsp	3	0.22
Pig's blood	1½ cups	313	20.00
Coppa di Testa, diced	8 oz	173	12.73
Beef middles or bung, rinsed			

This is an unsmoked variation on bologna that uses pork blood in place of water. You can order pig's blood from any good butcher shop. Often it will come frozen, which is fine; in that case, rather than freezing it as indicated in step 5 of the recipe, you'll want to let it thaw until it has a slush-like consistency.

1. Place the pork shoulder and bacon on a rimmed baking sheet, transfer to the freezer, and chill until crunchy on the exterior but not frozen solid (see page 23).

2. In a small bowl, add the milk powder, salt, mustard powder, black pepper, coriander, and Cure No. 1 and stir to combine.

3. Nest a large mixing bowl in a bowl filled with ice. Grind the meat through the small die of the grinder into the bowl set in ice (see page 24).

4. Add the spice mixture to the meat and stir with your hands until well incorporated; the mixture will look homogenous and will begin sticking to the bowl (see page 25).

5. Press a sheet of parchment paper or plastic wrap directly on the surface of the meat to prevent oxidation, then cover the bowl tightly with plastic wrap and refrigerate overnight. Alternatively, you can vacuum-seal the farce.

6. Pour the blood into a shallow baking dish, transfer to the freezer, and chill until semi-frozen, about 40 minutes.

7. Transfer the meat to the bowl of a food processor, add half of the semi-frozen blood and process until the liquid is incorporated into the meat and the mixture begins to look sticky, 1 to 2 minutes. Add the remaining blood and continue processing until the mixture is smooth, 4 to 5 minutes longer. Note: The temperature of your meat during this mixing step is critically important. Its temperature should never rise above 40°F/4°C; work efficiently during this step of the process. Depending on the size of your food processor, you may need to do this step in batches. Do not overload your machine or it will not work efficiently. Once fully puréed, gently fold in the coppa di testa.

8. Spoon 2 tbsp of the meat mixture into a nonstick frying pan and spread into a thin patty. Cook the test patty over low heat until cooked through but not browned. Taste the sausage for seasoning and adjust as necessary.

9. Stuff the sausage into the beef middles or bung (see page 36); the bologna should be about 5 in/12 cm in diameter and 10 in/25 cm long. Poach the bologna (see page 41) until the internal temperature reaches 155°F/68°C. Let it hang at room temperature until cool, then wrap tightly in plastic wrap and refrigerate overnight. It will keep, tightly wrapped or vacuum-sealed and refrigerated, for 1 week.

CHICKEN-BEER SAUSAGE

YIELD: 3 LB/1.4 KG

	U.S. MEASUREMENT	GRAMS	% OF TOTAL (100%)
Boneless, skin-on chicken thighs, cut into 1-in/2.5-cm cubes	3.90 lb	1,044	76.65
Lager-style beer	¾ cup	157	11.50
Eggs	2	62	4.55
Heavy cream	¼ cup	57	2.50
Fine sea salt	2 tbsp	45	2.00
Finely diced dried apricots	1½ tbsp	22	1.60
Whole mustard seeds	2 tsp	8	0.60
Coarsely ground black pepper	1 tsp	5	0.35
Whole fennel seeds	¾ tsp	3	0.25
Hog casings, rinsed			

This is the first sausage I developed, back before I opened 4505 Meats. Based on a boudin blanc, it has a fluffy texture, which I achieve by whipping the sausage farce in an electric mixer until it's creamy and light. I use chicken thighs and skin, which makes a juicy sausage, and I add diced dried apricots because I think the sweet-tart flavor cuts the richness of the meat. As for the beer, we use the Blue Bell Bitter from Magnolia Pub, a small brewery in San Francisco's Haight-Ashbury neighborhood. It's light but flavorful, and not too hoppy or bitter, which would overpower the delicate flavor of the chicken.

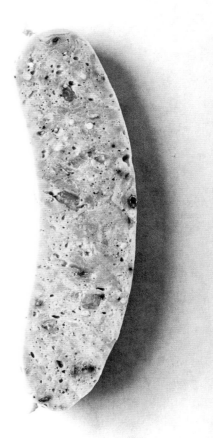

1. Place the chicken on a rimmed baking sheet, transfer to the freezer, and chill until crunchy on the exterior but not frozen solid (see page 23).

2. In a medium bowl, add the beer, eggs, cream, salt, apricots, mustard seeds, black pepper, and fennel seeds and set aside.

3. Nest a large mixing bowl in a bowl filled with ice. Grind the chicken through the small die of the grinder into the bowl set in ice (see page 24).

4. Add the beer mixture to the meat and stir with your hands until well incorporated; the mixture will look homogenous and will begin sticking to the bowl (see page 25).

5. Transfer the meat to the bowl of an electric mixer fitted with the paddle attachment and mix on medium speed until fluffy and creamy, about 4 minutes.

6. Spoon 2 tbsp of the meat mixture into a nonstick frying pan and spread into a thin patty. Cook the test patty over low heat until cooked through but not browned. Taste the sausage for seasoning and adjust as necessary.

7. Press a sheet of parchment paper or plastic wrap directly on the surface of the meat to prevent oxidation, then cover the bowl tightly with plastic wrap and refrigerate overnight. Alternatively, you can vacuum-seal the farce.

8. Stuff the sausage into the hog casings (see page 31) and twist into links (see page 36).

9. Poach the links (see page 41) in a light beer, such as a lager or pale ale, until an instant-read thermometer inserted in the center of a sausage registers 150°F/65°C. Eat immediately, or chill them fully in an ice water bath and refrigerate, or freeze for longer storage (see page 46). When you're ready to eat the sausages, grill them or cook in a pan until browned and heated through.

FOIE GRAS BOUDIN BLANC

YIELD: 3 LB/1.4 KG

	U.S. MEASUREMENT	GRAMS	% OF TOTAL (100%)
Boneless pork shoulder (or a combination of cuts, about 75% lean, 25% fat), cut into 1-in/2.5-cm cubes	1.70 lb	741	54.39
Beaten eggs	2	90	6.61
Nonfat dry milk powder	⅓ cup	68	5.00
Heavy cream	¼ cup	54	4.00
Fine sea salt	1 tbsp	31	2.30
Mustard powder	2¼ tsp	5	0.40
Ground anise	2 tsp	4	0.30
Black pepper	1½ tsp	3	0.20
Ground coriander	½ tsp	1	0.10
Cure No. 1 (see page 15)	½ tsp	3	0.04
Crushed ice	1 cup	204	15.00
Goose or duck foie gras, cleaned and cut into ¾-in/2-cm cubes	0.40 lb	159	11.66
Hog casings, rinsed			

This is a classic sausage with a political agenda. In the summer of 2012, the State of California banned the production and sale of foie gras, the fattened livers of duck and geese, on grounds of animal cruelty (the animals are force fed to fatten their livers, a time-honored French technique called *gavage*). Before the ban took effect we wanted to showcase foie gras one last time with this sausage, a rich boudin blanc studded with cubes of creamy, rich foie gras. We cut the foie gras into larger cubes so it doesn't melt away; you want to see (and taste) it in each bite.

1. Place the pork on a rimmed baking sheet, transfer to the freezer, and chill until crunchy on the exterior but not frozen solid (see page 23).

2. In a small bowl, add the eggs, milk powder, cream, salt, mustard powder, anise, black pepper, coriander, and Cure No. 1 and stir to combine.

3. Nest a large mixing bowl in a bowl filled with ice. Grind the meat through the small die of the grinder into the bowl set in ice (see page 24).

4. Add the spice mixture to the meat and stir with your hands until well incorporated; the mixture will look homogenous and will begin sticking to the bowl (see page 25).

5. Press a sheet of parchment paper or plastic wrap directly onto the surface of the meat to prevent oxidation, then cover the bowl tightly with plastic wrap and refrigerate overnight. Alternatively, you can vacuum-seal the farce.

6. Transfer the meat to the bowl of a food processor, add half of the crushed ice and process until the liquid is incorporated into the meat and the mixture begins to look sticky, 1 to 2 minutes. Add the remaining crushed ice and continue processing until smooth, 4 to 5 minutes longer. Note: The temperature of your meat during this mixing step is critically important. Its temperature should never rise above 40°F/4°C; work efficiently during this step of the process. Depending on the size of your food processor, you may need to do this in batches. Fold in the foie gras.

CONTINUED

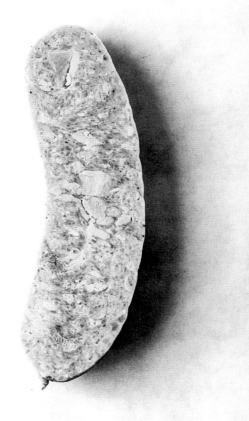

7. Spoon 2 tbsp of the meat mixture into a nonstick frying pan and spread into a thin patty. Cook the test patty over low heat until cooked through but not browned. Taste the sausage for seasoning and adjust as necessary.

8. Stuff the sausage into the hog casings (see page 31) and twist into links (see page 36).

9. Poach these sausages (see page 41) in water or an off-dry (slightly sweet) white wine until an instant-read thermometer inserted in the center of a sausages registers 148°F/65°C. They can be eaten immediately, or chill them fully in an ice-water bath and refrigerate, or freeze for longer storage (see page 46). When you're ready to eat the sausages, cook them on a grill or in a pan until browned and heated through.

LAMB WIENERS

....

YIELD: 3 LB/1.4 KG

	U.S. MEASUREMENT	GRAMS	% OF TOTAL (100%)
Boneless lamb shoulder (or a combination of cuts, about 75% lean, 25% fat), cut into 1-in/2.5-cm cubes	1.30 lb	574	42.11
Lamb hard fat, cut into 1-in/2.5-cm cubes	⅓ cup	70	5.14
Boneless lean beef, such as round, sirloin, neck, plate or shank (about 95% lean, 5% fat) cut into 1-in/2.5-cm cubes	0.90 lb	420	30.81
Chopped Garlic Confit (page 182)	3 tbsp	28	2.05
Fine sea salt	1 tbsp	25	1.85
Fennel seeds	2¼ tsp	6	0.41
Finely chopped fresh rosemary leaves	1 tbsp	5	0.38
Coarsely ground black pepper	¾ tsp	3	0.21
Onion powder	¾ tsp	2	0.13
Cure No. 1 (see page 15)	½ tsp	3	0.06
Crushed ice	1 cup	230	16.85
Sheep casings, rinsed			

Lamb is often seasoned with garlic and rosemary, so when I set about making this sausage I began with that classic flavor profile. The additional lamb fat in this recipe makes it exceptionally rich and juicy. You should be able to purchase hard lamb fat from any butcher; if you're utilizing the whole animal, use the fat surrounding the kidneys, in the neck, and on the belly.

1. Place the lamb shoulder, lamb fat, and beef on a rimmed baking sheet, transfer to the freezer, and chill until crunchy on the exterior but not frozen solid (see page 23).

2. In a small bowl, add the garlic confit, salt, fennel seeds, rosemary, black pepper, onion powder, and Cure No. 1 and stir to combine.

3. Nest a large mixing bowl in a bowl filled with ice. Grind the meat through the small die of the grinder into the bowl set in ice (see page 24).

4. Add the spice mixture to the meat and stir with your hands until well incorporated; the mixture will look homogenous and will begin sticking to the bowl (see page 25).

5. Press a sheet of parchment paper or plastic wrap directly on the surface of the meat to prevent oxidation, then cover the bowl tightly with plastic wrap and refrigerate overnight. Alternatively, you can vacuum-seal the farce.

6. Transfer the meat to the bowl of a food processor, add half the crushed ice and process until all of the ice has dissolved, 1 to 2 minutes. Add the remaining crushed ice and continue processing until the mixture is completely smooth, 4 to 5 minutes longer. Note: The temperature of your meat during this mixing step is critically important. Its temperature should never rise above 40°F/4°C; work efficiently during this step of the process.

7. Spoon 2 tbsp of the meat mixture into a nonstick frying pan and spread into a thin patty. Cook the test patty over low heat until cooked through but not browned. Taste the sausage for seasoning and adjust as necessary.

8. Stuff the sausage into the sheep casings (see page 31) and twist into links (see page 36).

9. Smoke the links (see page 43) at 170°F/77°C, until the internal temperature of the sausage reaches 145°F/63°C, 45 to 60 minutes. Remove the sausages from the smoker, let cool slightly, then transfer to a refrigerator and let stand, uncovered, overnight. The following day, the wieners can be heated through in a pan or on a grill.

LIVERWURST

YIELD: 3 LB/1.4 KG

	U.S. MEASUREMENT	GRAMS	% OF TOTAL (100%)
Boneless pork shoulder (or a combination of pork cuts, about 75% lean, 25% fat), cut into 1-in/2.5-cm cubes	1.20 lb	550	40.36
Pork liver, cut into 1-in/2.5-cm cubes	0.60 lb	298	21.90
Heavy cream	2 cups + 2 tbsp	280	20.54
Eggs	2	90	6.61
Crème frâiche	¼ cup	52	3.81
All-purpose flour	⅓ cup	24	1.73
Madeira	2 tbsp	35	2.57
Fine sea salt	1½ tsp	13	0.99
Fresh thyme leaves	1 tbsp + 1½ tsp	7	0.49
Coarsely ground black pepper	1 tbsp	7	0.49
Ground coriander	1 tbsp	5	0.35
Ground nutmeg	½ tsp	1	0.06
Cure No. 1 (see page 15)	½ tsp	3	0.10
Beef middles, rinsed			

My favorite way to eat liverwurst is on a cracker, topped with slivered yellow onion. Though pork liver is high in protein, it isn't a great binder, so I add a small amount of flour to the farce to make the liverwurst smooth and spreadable.

1. Place the pork shoulder and liver on a rimmed baking sheet, transfer to the freezer, and chill until crunchy on the exterior but not frozen solid (see page 23).

2. In a medium bowl, add the cream, eggs, crème frâiche, flour, Madeira, salt, thyme, black pepper, coriander, nutmeg, and Cure No. 1 and stir to combine.

3. Nest a large mixing bowl in a bowl filled with ice. Grind the meat and liver through the small die of the grinder into the bowl set in ice (see page 24).

4. Add the cream mixture to the meat and stir with your hands until well incorporated; the mixture will look homogenous and will begin sticking to the bowl (see page 25).

5. Transfer the meat to the bowl of a food processor and process until the mixture is completely smooth, 5 to 6 minutes. Note: The temperature of your meat during this mixing step is critically important. Its temperature should never rise about 40°F/4°C; work efficiently during this step of the process. Depending on the size of your food processor, you may need to do this in batches.

6. Spoon 2 tbsp of the meat mixture into a nonstick frying pan and spread into a thin patty. Cook the test patty over low heat until cooked through but not browned. Taste the sausage for seasoning and adjust as necessary.

7. Press a sheet of parchment paper or plastic wrap directly on the surface of the meat to prevent oxidation, then cover the bowl tightly with plastic wrap and refrigerate overnight. Alternatively, you can vacuum-seal the farce.

8. Stuff the sausage into the beef middles (see page 31), twist, and tie off with kitchen twine (see page 36) into six links, each about 5 in/12.5 cm long.

9. Smoke the liverwurst (see page 43) at 170°F/77°C, until the internal temperature of the sausage reaches 145°F/63°C, about 90 minutes.

10. Remove the liverwurst from the smoker and immediately transfer the links to a cooling rack. Let stand until completely cool. Vacuum-seal the links or tightly wrap each link individually in plastic wrap and refrigerate overnight. Vacuum-sealed links will keep several weeks. If wrapped in plastic, they should be eaten within 1 week.

SMOKED TROUT AND PORK SAUSAGE

YIELD: 3 LB/1.4 KG

	U.S. MEASUREMENT	GRAMS	% OF TOTAL (100%)
Boneless pork shoulder (or a combination of pork cuts, about 75% lean, 25% fat), cut into 1-in/2.5-cm cubes	1.00 lb	439	32.25
Fine sea salt	2 tbsp	41	3.00
Eggs	2	90	6.61
Nonfat dry milk powder	½ cup	82	6.00
Crème fraîche	¼ cup	87	6.39
Freshly grated horseradish	1 tbsp	10	0.75
Coarsely ground black pepper	1½ tsp	4	0.30
Ground coriander	1½ tsp	4	0.30
Smoked trout, skin removed	0.40 lb	185	13.60
Crushed ice	4 cups	409	30.00
Finely diced red onion	2 tbsp	4	0.30
Finely chopped fresh parsley	2 tbsp	7	0.50
Hog casings, rinsed			

This is everything I like about eating smoked fish, in tube form. Serve this sausage with greens and Horseradish and Black Pepper Crema (page 186) or, for an uptown hors d'oeuvre, slice it into coins and serve on blinis, topped with more crème frâiche and a dollop of caviar.

1. Place the pork on a rimmed baking sheet, transfer to the freezer, and chill until crunchy on the exterior but not frozen solid (see page 23).

2. In a small bowl, combine the salt, eggs, milk powder, crème frâiche, horseradish, black pepper, and coriander and stir to combine.

3. Nest a large mixing bowl in a bowl filled with ice. Grind the meat and fat through the small die of the grinder into the bowl set in ice (see page 24). Place the trout on the baking sheet and chill in the freezer until crunchy on the exterior but not frozen solid.

4. Add the spice mixture to the meat and stir with your hands until well incorporated; the mixture will look homogenous and will begin sticking to the bowl (see page 25).

5. Transfer the meat to the bowl of a food processor, add half the ice and process until all of the ice has dissolved, 1 to 2 minutes. Add the remaining ice and continue processing until the mixture is completely smooth, 4 to 5 minutes. Note: The temperature of your meat during this mixing step is critically important. Its temperature should never rise about 40°F/4°C; work efficiently during this step of the process. Remove the trout from the freezer and chop.

6. Spoon 2 tbsp of the meat mixture into a nonstick frying pan and spread into a thin patty. Cook the test patty over low heat until cooked through but not browned. Taste the sausage for seasoning and adjust as necessary. Once satisfied with the flavor, fold in the chopped trout, red onion, and parsley.

7. Press a sheet of parchment paper or plastic wrap directly on the surface of the meat to prevent oxidation, then cover the bowl tightly with plastic wrap and refrigerate overnight. Alternatively, you can vacuum-seal the farce.

8. Stuff the sausage into the hog casings (see page 31) and twist into links (see page 36).

9. Smoke the links (see page 43) at 170°F/77°C, until the internal temperature of the sausage reaches 145°F/63°C, 45 to 60 minutes. Remove the sausages from the smoker, let cool slightly, then transfer to a refrigerator and let stand, uncovered, overnight. When you're ready to eat the sausages, they can be cooked on a grill (see page 38) until heated through.

CHAPTER 6

COMBI-
NATION
SAUSAGE

chicken and egg galantine

veal, sweetbreads,
and morels en croute

truffled boudin en croute

duck confit and
cherry terrine

pig's head terrine

If the previous chapters haven't convinced you of the glorious possibilities of sausage, this chapter ought to seal the deal. Once you've mastered basic sausage making, the next step is to move on to some of these more involved recipes for pastry-wrapped terrines and sausage-stuffed suckling pig.

These recipes are rooted in classical French technique, but they've unfortunately fallen out of fashion; it's difficult to find well-made ballotines and galantines, though they were once a butcher-shop staple. Most of the recipes in this chapter use at least one of the sausage recipes from earlier in the book; instead of casing the farce (or cooking it loose), these are some other suggestions for what you can do with sausage.

Admittedly, these aren't the simplest recipes, so plan to attempt them when you have both time and patience; I consider them to be special-occasion preparations, suited to festive gatherings when you've got some guests with hearty appetites.

CHICKEN AND EGG GALANTINE

YIELD: ONE 8-LB/17.6-KG GALANTINE

	U.S. MEASUREMENT	GRAMS	% OF TOTAL (100%)
Boneless, skin-on chicken thighs, cut into 1-in/2.5-cm cubes	1.10 lb	519	14.28
Boneless, skin-on chicken breast meat, cut into 1-in/2.5-cm cubes	0.80 lb	361	9.93
Pork back fat, cut into 1-in/2.5-cm cubes	⅓ cup	84	2.31
Ice water	2 tbsp	33	0.90
White wine	2 tbsp	25	0.69
Minced chervil	2 tbsp	6	0.17
Fine sea salt	1½ tsp	14	0.39
Finely ground black pepper	1 tsp	2	0.07
Fava beans, shelled and peeled	½ cup	63	1.72
Olive oil	1 tbsp	13	0.40
Finely diced porcini mushrooms	½ cup	63	1.72
Whole chicken	5.00 lb	857	62.25
Eggs, hardboiled	4	145	5.17

When you slice into this galantine—a whole, deboned chicken stuffed with a chicken sausage—you see a beautiful mosaic: the chicken sausage, studded with brilliant green fava beans, flecked with porcini mushrooms, and a golden-yolked hard-cooked egg in the center. This would make an elegant first course.

1. Place the chicken thigh and breast meat and pork fat on a rimmed baking sheet, transfer to the freezer, and chill until crunchy on the exterior but not frozen solid (see page 23).

2. In a small bowl, add the water, wine, chervil, salt, and black pepper and stir to combine.

3. Nest a large mixing bowl in a bowl filled with ice. Grind the meat, skin, and pork fat through the small die of the grinder into the bowl set in ice (see page 24).

4. Add the water and herb mixture to the meat and stir with your hands until well incorporated; the mixture will look homogenous and will begin sticking to the bowl (see page 25).

5. Spoon 2 tbsp of the meat mixture into a nonstick frying pan and spread into a thin patty. Cook the test patty over low heat until cooked through but not browned. Taste the sausage for seasoning and adjust as necessary.

6. Fill a medium bowl with ice and water. Bring a small saucepan of salted water to a boil, then add the fava beans and cook just until tender, about 2 minutes. Drain the fava beans and transfer to the ice bath. When cool, remove favas from the ice bath and drain on paper towels. Set aside.

7. In a small sauté pan over medium heat, heat the olive oil. Add the mushrooms and cook, stirring, until golden brown and soft, about 5 minutes. Remove from the heat and set aside.

8. When the mushrooms have cooled, gently fold them and the fava beans into the farce.

9. Press a sheet of parchment paper or plastic wrap directly on the surface of the meat to prevent oxidation, then cover the bowl tightly with plastic wrap and refrigerate overnight. Alternatively, you can vacuum-seal the farce.

10. Place the whole chicken on a work surface, breast-side down, and remove the wishbone **(A)**. Cut through the skin along the backbone, from neck to tail. Working to the left and right along the backbone **(B)**, separate the meat from the carcass and fold open, running your knife between the breastbone and skin **(C)**. Continue cutting downward on either side of the backbone until you have freed the backbone, rib cage, and breastbone, taking care not to puncture the skin.

11. Carefully lift out the carcass (discard or save for stock); the leg and wing bones remain on the chicken. Position the chicken flat on your work surface and remove the thigh bones **(D)**. Begin to thread kitchen string through the skin and thigh meat **(E)**. Season with salt **(F)**.

12. Remove the sausage farce from the refrigerator and spoon inside the deboned chicken, spreading it into an even layer down the center. Arrange the whole hardboiled eggs in a straight line down the center **(G)**.

13. Pull the skin of the chicken together from each side **(H)**. With a trussing needle, sew up the chicken skin from tail to neck **(I)**. With your hands, re-form the chicken as closely as possible to its original shape, then firmly truss the bird so that the legs and wings are tightly secured to the body **(J, K)**. Weigh the galantine and make note of the number (to determine the cooking time in step 15).

CONTINUED

14. Tightly wrap the chicken with cheesecloth, securing the ends **(L)**, or vacuum-seal the entire galantine. Bring a large pot of water or chicken stock to a boil over high heat, then reduce the heat so that the liquid is simmering. When the liquid registers 176°F/80°C on an instant-read thermometer, gently lower the chicken into the pot **(M)**.

15. Cook the galantine, uncovered, maintaining the temperature of the liquid at 176°F/80°C, for 20 minutes per 1 lb/455 g, until a thermometer inserted into the center of the galantine registers 152°F/67°C. Carefully remove the galantine **(N)**. Transfer to a wire rack set over a rimmed baking sheet. When completely cool, cut away the cheesecloth **(O)**. Refrigerate overnight. The following day, slice; serve cool or at room temperature.

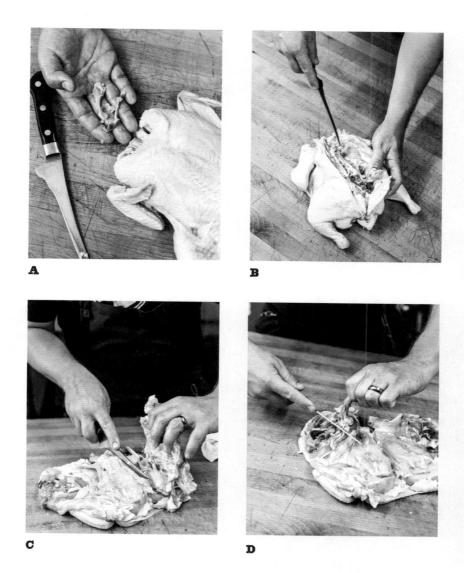

A

B

C

D

E

F

G

K

L

M

H

I

J

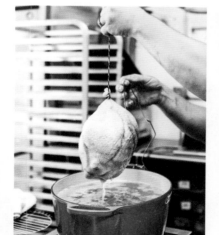

N

O

DUCK CONFIT AND CHERRY TERRINE

YIELD: ONE 3-LB/1.4-KG TERRINE

	U.S. MEASUREMENT	GRAMS	% OF TOTAL (100%)
Boneless, skin-on duck thighs, cut into 1-in/2.5-cm cubes	1.40 lb	635	46.59
Boneless prepared duck confit, cut into 1-in/2.5-cm cubes	1.00 lb	453	33.28
Dried cherries, coarsely chopped	1 cup	147	10.78
Water	1 tbsp	59	4.31
Port wine	1 tbsp	44	3.24
Fine sea salt	1½ tsp	15	1.08
Ground nutmeg	1 tsp	2	0.14
Ground anise	1 tsp	2	0.14
Ground cinnamon	½ tsp	1	0.07
Coarsely ground black pepper	1½ tsp	4	0.30
Ground cloves	½ tsp	1	0.07
Thinly sliced lardo or pork back fat for lining the terrine mold, about 0.50 lb/227 g			

This terrine is perfect for the winter months. The sweetness of the port-plumped cherries offsets the richness of the duck and duck confit; anise, cinnamon, nutmeg, and cloves give it a particularly festive flavor. Prepared duck confit—legs and thighs that have been slowly poached in duck fat—is available at well-stocked butcher shops as well as online at D'Artagnan (www.dartagnan.com).

1. Place the duck thigh meat and cooked confit on a rimmed baking sheet, transfer to the freezer, and chill until crunchy on the exterior but not frozen solid (see page 23).

2. Put the cherries in a small bowl and add the water and port. In a second small bowl, add the salt, nutmeg, anise, cinnamon, black pepper, and cloves and stir to combine.

3. Nest a large mixing bowl in a bowl filled with ice. Grind the duck thighs through the small die of the grinder into the bowl set in ice (see page 24).

4. Add the cherries and liquid and the dry spice mixture to the meat and stir with your hands until well incorporated; the mixture will look homogenous and will begin sticking to the bowl (see page 25). Fold in the duck confit.

5. Spoon 2 tbsp of the meat mixture into a nonstick frying pan and spread into a thin patty. Cook the test patty over low heat until cooked through but not browned. Taste the sausage for seasoning and adjust as necessary.

6. Press a sheet of parchment paper or plastic wrap directly on the surface of the meat to prevent oxidation, then cover the bowl tightly with plastic wrap and refrigerate overnight. Alternatively, you can vacuum-seal the farce.

7. Line a 3-lb-/1.4-kg-capacity and 12-by-3-by-3.25-in/30.5-by-7.5-by-8-cm terrine mold with plastic wrap, leaving ample overhang on each side (this will make it easier to lift the finished terrine out of the pan) (**A**). Line the mold with some of the sliced lardo slightly overlapping the slices (**B**).

8. Preheat the oven to 300°F/150°C. Spoon the farce into the prepared mold, packing it in tightly and smoothing the top (**C**). Gently bang the bottom of the terrine mold on your work surface to eliminate air bubbles in the farce. Place the remaining lardo on the surface of the terrine (**D**), then wrap the overhanging plastic over the top of the terrine (**E**).

9. Transfer the terrine to a water bath (**F**). Cook for 2 hours, until the internal temperature registers 145°F/63°C. Prepare an ice-water bath. Remove the water bath from the oven, then carefully remove the terrine from the water bath and pour off any fat that has accumulated on the surface (**G**). Transfer the terrine to the ice water (**H**). Let cool to room temperature, replenishing the ice as necessary, then remove from the ice-water bath. Weight the surface of the terrine (a brick wrapped in foil or a large can works well for this purpose) (**I**). Transfer to the refrigerator. Refrigerate for at least 8 hours or overnight.

10. When you're ready to serve the terrine, use the plastic wrap to gently lift the terrine from the mold. Carefully unwrap and discard the plastic wrap, then slice the terrine into thin slices and serve cool or at room temperature.

CONTINUED

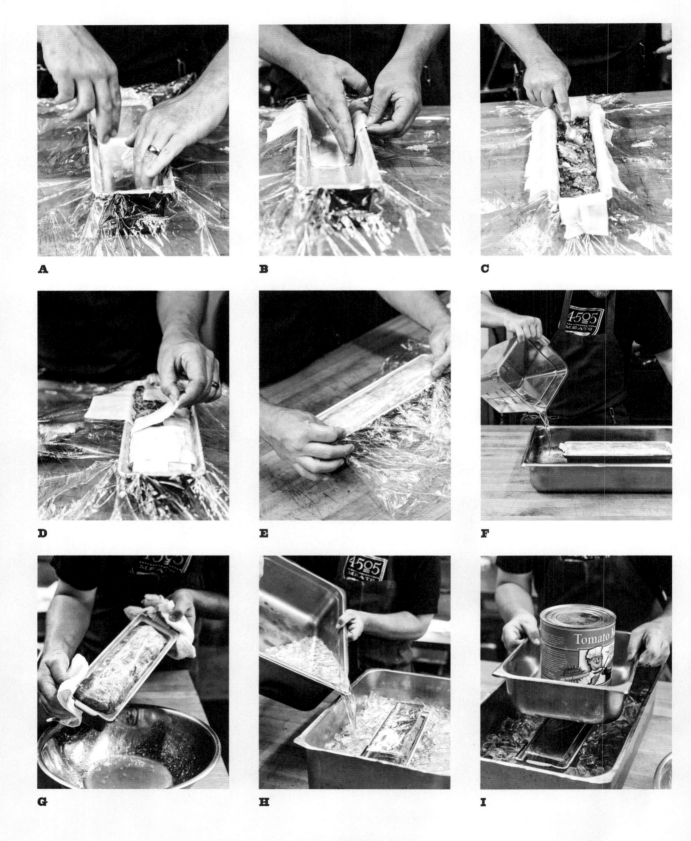

A   B   C

D   E   F

G   H   I

TRUFFLED BOUDIN EN CROUTE

....

YIELD: ONE 3-LB./1.4-KG TERRINE

	U.S. MEASUREMENT	GRAMS	% OF TOTAL (100%)
Boneless, skin-on duck breast	2 breasts	409	27.95
Fine sea salt	1½ tsp	10	0.75
Pie Pastry (page 151)	0.50 lb	195	14.29
Egg wash (1 egg beaten with 1 tbsp water)	—	—	—
Foie Gras Boudin Blanc (page 122), raw, uncased	1.50 lb	610	44.76
Finely sliced black truffle	1 tbsp	25	1.83
Gelatin sheets	1 sheet	3	0.22
Sauternes	⅔ cup	139	10.20

I absolutely love *en croute* preparations, where a meaty filling is enclosed in buttery, golden pastry. This is an especially luxurious version: foie gras–studded boudin blanc is further enhanced by chopped black truffles, then accented with duck breast, and wrapped in dough. The Sauternes gelée is a perfect finishing touch. A hinged pâté mold makes unmolding the finished terrine easy. This would make a perfect first course for a festive holiday feast.

1. Season the duck breast with the salt. Place a medium cast-iron skillet over medium-high heat and add the duck breast, skin-side down. Cook, turning once, until the internal temperature registers 137°F/58°C on an instant-read thermometer. Remove from the pan and let cool completely, then slice. Set aside.

2. Preheat the oven to 350°F/180°C. Roll the pie pastry into a large rectangle about ⅛ in/3 mm thick. Using a 3-lb-/1.4-kg-capacity and 12-by-3-by-3¼-in/30.5-by-7.5-by-8-cm hinged pâté mold or similar terrine mold to guide you, cut the pastry to fit the mold with about ½ in/12 mm of overhang on all sides; cut one piece of dough to form the lid. Use a small round pastry cutter to cut two holes in the lid piece and, if desired, cut two decorative rounds of dough for the vents (**A**).

3. Lightly butter the inside of the terrine mold, then transfer the dough carefully to the mold (**B**). Gently press so that the dough adheres to the sides of the terrine mold; if necessary, patch any holes or corners. Trim the overhang so that it's even on all sides. Brush the egg wash along the creases of the dough to seal (**C**).

4. Fill the dough-lined terrine mold by layering the boudin blanc, truffle, boudin blanc, duck breast, and boudin blanc to finish, smoothing the top (**D**). Bang the mold on the work surface to eliminate air bubbles. Fold the dough overhang over the top of terrine to begin to form the lid, pressing gently.

5. Brush the pastry on the top of the terrine with some of the egg wash (**E**). Lay the lid piece of dough on top of the terrine, pressing gently so that it adheres to the egg-washed pastry beneath. Press any overhanging edges down inside the mold and place the decorative dough circles on the vents (**F**).

6. Cut two pieces of foil into rectangles, about 6 in/15 cm long by 4 in/10 cm wide. Fold each rectangle in half lengthwise, then roll into a tube. Place one tube in each of the holes that you have cut in the surface of the terrine (**G**); this will allow steam to escape without marring the surface of the terrine.

7. Brush the entire surface of the pastry lid with the remaining egg wash, then transfer the terrine to the oven and bake for 1 hour 15 minutes, or until the terrine reaches an internal temperature of 145°F/63°C (insert the thermometer in one of the foil chimneys to check) and the top is nicely browned.

CONTINUED

8. Remove from the oven and let stand at room temperature for 30 minutes. Carefully pour out the rendered fat and juice (**H**). Transfer to the refrigerator overnight.

9. The next day, soak the gelatin sheet in cold water for 5 to 10 minutes. Gently heat the Sauternes in a small saucepan over low heat (do not let it boil), then wring out the gelatin sheet and add to the Sauternes, stirring until completely dissolved. Remove from the heat and let the mixture cool slightly. Remove the terrine from the refrigerator and carefully pour the Sauternes through the chimneys, dividing evenly (**I**). Return the terrine to the refrigerator and refrigerate overnight. When you're ready to eat the terrine, carefully unmold it on a cutting board and cut with a sharp knife into thin slices.

A

B

C

D

E

F

G

H

I

PIE PASTRY

YIELD: 1 LB/455 G

	U.S. MEASUREMENT	GRAMS	% OF TOTAL (100%)
All-purpose flour	3¾ cups	236	52.08
Cold butter or lard, cut into small cubes	1 cup	118	26.04
Fine sea salt	¾ tsp	5	1.05
Water	⅔ cup	95	20.83

1. Sift the flour onto your work surface and make a well in the center. Put the cubed butter and salt in the well. Using a pastry cutter or your fingertips, rub the butter into the flour until it resembles coarse meal.

2. Sprinkle the water over the flour-and-fat mixture and shape the dough into a ball. Knead briefly until the dough holds together, then wrap tightly in plastic wrap and refrigerate for at least 1 hour before using.

PIG'S HEAD TERRINE

··

YIELD: ONE 3-LB/1.4-KG TERRINE

	U.S. MEASUREMENT	GRAMS	% OF TOTAL (100%)
Cooked pig's head, trotter, and shank meat (see page 55), bones removed, and roughly chopped into bite-size pieces	0.50 lb	271	19.94
Boneless pork shoulder, cut into 1-in/2.5-cm cubes	2.00 lb	776	57.00
Pistachios, toasted	½ cup	61	4.45
Water	1 tbsp	105	7.70
White wine	1 tbsp	12	0.90
Fine sea salt	1½ tsp	10	0.75
Finely chopped charred green onions	⅓ cup	18	1.35
Red pepper flakes	1 tsp	2	0.15
Coarsely ground black pepper	2¼ tsp	4	0.30
Finely chopped fresh parsley	¼ cup	12	0.90
Cure No. 1 (see page 15)	¼ tsp	1	0.11
Dried prunes, chopped	¼ cup	88	6.45
Caul fat or thinly sliced pork back fat for lining the terrine mold, about 0.50 lb/227 g			

Like headcheese, this terrine relies on the collagen-rich meat from a cooked pig's head, trotters, and shank, combined with pork shoulder. Because these cuts are already very flavorful, I season the terrine simply. This recipe includes charred green onions. Char them on a gas or charcoal grill or cook them in a cast-iron pan until soft and blackened in spots.

1. Place the pork shoulder, head, trotter, and shank meat on a rimmed baking sheet, transfer to the freezer, and chill until crunchy on the exterior but not frozen solid (see page 23).

2. In a small bowl add the pistachios, water, wine, salt, green onions, red pepper flakes, black pepper, parsley, Cure No. 1, and prunes and mix well to combine.

3. Nest a large mixing bowl in a bowl filled with ice. Grind the pork meat into the bowl set in ice (see page 24).

4. Add the pistachio mixture to the ground pork and stir with your hands until well incorporated; the mixture will look homogenous and will begin sticking to the bowl (see page 25).

5. Spoon 2 tbsp of the meat mixture into a nonstick frying pan and spread into a thin patty. Cook the test patty over low heat until cooked through but not browned. Taste the sausage for seasoning and adjust as necessary.

6. Press a sheet of parchment paper or plastic wrap directly on the surface of the meat to prevent oxidation, then cover the bowl tightly with plastic wrap and refrigerate overnight. Alternatively, you can vacuum-seal the farce.

7. Line a 3-lb-/1.4-kg-capacity and 12-by-3-by-3¼-in/30.5-by-7.5-by-8-cm terrine mold with plastic wrap, leaving ample overhang on each side (this will make it easier to lift the finished terrine out of the mold.) Line the mold with some of the caul fat or back fat.

8. Preheat the oven to 300°F/150°C. Spoon the farce into the prepared mold, packing it in tightly and smoothing the top. Gently bang the bottom of the terrine mold on your work surface to eliminate air bubbles in the farce. Place the remaining caul fat or back fat on the surface of the terrine, then wrap the overhanging plastic wrap over the top of the terrine.

9. Transfer the terrine to a water bath and cook for 2 hours, until the internal temperature registers 145°F/63°C. As the terrine cooks, prepare an ice-water bath. Remove the water bath from the oven, then carefully remove the terrine from the water bath, pour off any excess fat that has accumulated on the surface, and transfer the terrine to the ice-water bath. Let cool to room temperature, replenishing the ice as necessary, then remove from the ice-water bath. Weight the surface of the terrine (a brick wrapped in foil works well for this purpose) and transfer to the refrigerator. Refrigerate for at least 8 hours or overnight.

10. When you're ready to serve the terrine, use the plastic wrap to gently lift the terrine from the mold. Carefully unwrap and discard the plastic wrap, then cut the terrine into thin slices and serve cool or at room temperature.

WHOLE SUCKLING PIG BALLOTINE

YIELD: APPROXIMATELY 25 LB/11 KG

	U.S. MEASUREMENT	GRAMS	% OF TOTAL (100%)
Bacon, thickly sliced	1.00 lb	437	3.21
Pig's Head Terrine farce, raw (see page 152)	3.00 lb	1,380	9.41
Whole suckling pig	24.00 lb	11,254	76.63
Fine sea salt	2 tbsp	58	0.42
Coarsely ground black pepper	¼ cup	19	0.14
Red pepper flakes	¼ cup	29	0.21
Brown sugar	2 tbsp	58	0.42
Coriander	¼ cup	19	0.14
Lao Sausage, raw (see page 78)	3.00 lb	1,380	9.41
Olive oil for drizzling			

Admittedly, not everyone is going to be up for the challenge of cooking an entire suckling pig. But for those who are, this is a show-stopping way to prepare it. The pig is first deboned, then stuffed with both Lao Sausage and the Pig's Head Terrine, before being rolled like a porchetta and roasted until the skin is as crispy as a potato chip. A slice of the finished ballotine will have a swath of pork meat, some of the sausage and terrine, and a piece of crunchy skin. Heaven.

1. Position a 14-in-/35.5-cm-long rectangle of plastic wrap on your work surface with a long side facing you. Arrange the sliced bacon crosswise on top of the plastic wrap, arranging the slices so that they are touching but not overlapping.

2. Form the pig's head farce into a cylinder, about 3 in/7.5 cm in diameter by 24 in/61 cm long, and position it, centered, on top of the bacon, with the long side facing you (**A**). Using the plastic wrap as a guide, tightly roll into a bacon-wrapped cylinder (**B, C**). Twist the ends of the plastic wrap to form a tight, even cylinder (**D**). Transfer to a rimmed baking sheet and place in the freezer until very cold but not frozen through, about 1 hour.

3. Lay the pig back-side down on your work surface. With the tip of your boning knife, make an incision along each rib, making sure not to cut through the belly meat (**E**). Cut through the cartilage of the ribs and the breast bone (**F**). Start to peel the belly from the ribs (**G, H**). Repeat on the other side (**I**). Keeping one side of your knife on the bone at all times, continue to remove all the meat from the bones, taking care not to cut through the skin (**J, K, L, M**). Once the skeleton has been removed from the meat, chop through the neck bone with a hatchet (or cleaver and mallet) to fully remove the whole skeleton while keeping the head attached (**N, O**). With the cleaver, cut through the end of the spine to remove the tail end and hind legs (**P**).

4. Preheat the oven to 450°F/230°C. Lay the deboned pig, skin-side down, on your work surface with the long side facing you. In a small bowl, add the salt, black pepper, red pepper flakes, brown sugar, and coriander and stir to combine. Sprinkle the mixture all over the flesh side of the pig (**Q**).

5. Using an offset spatula, spread the Lao sausage on the seasoned flesh side of the pig, spreading it into an even layer about 1 in/2.5 cm thick. Remove the terrine from the refrigerator. Remove the plastic wrap from the bacon-wrapped terrine. Place the farce on top of the layer of Lao sausage, centering it (**R**). Lift the side of the pig closest to you up and over the terrine, then begin rolling it away from you, as tightly as you are able, until you have a compact cylinder enclosing the terrine. Tightly tie the cylinder with butcher's twine at 2-in/5-cm intervals (**S, T, U, V**).

6. Transfer the pig to a wire rack set over a rimmed baking sheet, drizzle the skin with olive oil, and season with salt (**W, X**). Transfer to the oven and cook for 45 minutes, then reduce the oven temperature to 275°F/135°C and continue cooking until the skin is deeply browned and crisp and an instant-read thermometer inserted in the center of the pig registers 145°F/63°C, about 1½ hours longer.

7. Carefully remove the pan from the oven (a good deal of fat will have collected in the rimmed baking pan, which you don't want to spill) and let rest for 30 to 45 minutes. Transfer to a cutting board and slice into 1-in/2.5-cm slices. Serve warm.

CONTINUED

A

B

C

G

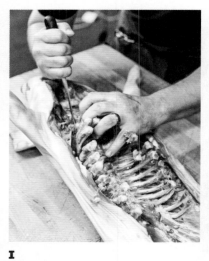

H

I

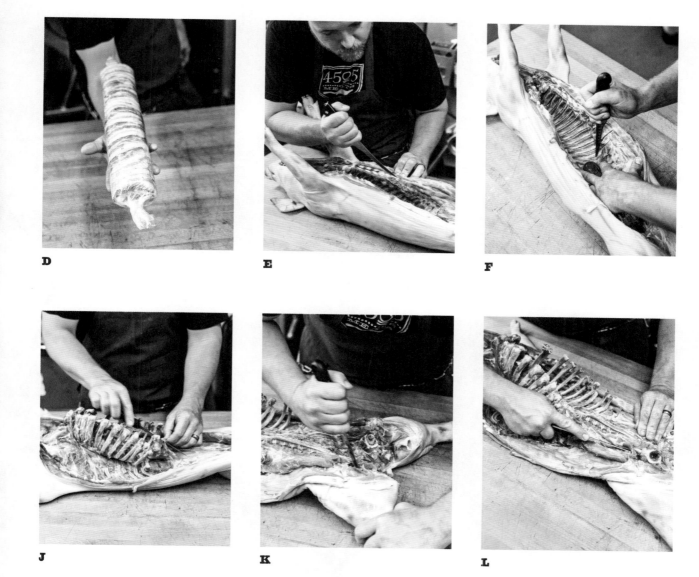

D

E

F

J

K

L

M

N

O

S

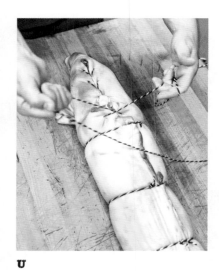

T

U

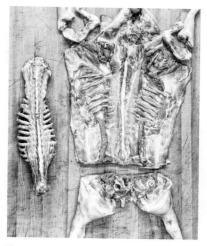

P

Q

R

V

W

X

VEAL, SWEETBREADS, AND MORELS EN CROUTE

YIELD: ONE 3-LB./1.4-KG TERRINE

	U.S. MEASUREMENT	GRAMS	% OF TOTAL (100%)
Veal sweetbreads, cleaned	⅔ cup	153	11.22
Veal stock	2 cups	—	—
Veal meat; 80% lean, 20% fat	1.20 lb	495	35.41
Egg	1	45	3.30
Nonfat dry milk powder	⅓ cup	52	3.46
Heavy cream	2 tbsp	37	2.49
Fine sea salt	1 tbsp	24	1.59
Fines herbes	¼ cup	15	1.02
Cure No. 1 (see page 15)	¼ tsp	1	0.11
Crushed ice	½ cup	151	10.07
Olive oil	1 tsp	4	0.25
Chopped morels	¼ cup	76	5.08
Dry vermouth	2 tbsp	19	1.27
Pie Pastry (page 151)	0.50 lb	195	14.29
Egg wash (1 egg beaten with 1 tbsp water)	—	—	—
Gelatin Sheets	1 sheet	3	0.22
Madeira	⅔ cup	139	10.22

Like the recipes in the Smooth Sausage chapter, this terrine contains an egg-and-cream-rich sausage farce that has been whipped in the food processor until light and smooth. The cooked, cubed sweetbreads and morels add both texture and flavor, and the golden pastry crust adds another element to this elegant presentation. The sweetbreads have to be cooked ahead and pressed overnight, so plan accordingly. For step-by-step photos showing how to assemble the terrine, see page 149.

1. Fill a medium saucepan halfway with water and bring to a simmer over medium-high heat. As the water comes to a simmer, prepare an ice-water bath. Add the sweetbreads to the saucepan, let the water return to a simmer, and then transfer the sweetbreads to the ice bath with a slotted spoon.

2. When the sweetbreads are completely cool, remove them from the ice bath and, with a sharp knife, peel the membrane from the exterior of the sweetbreads. Place a double thickness of paper towels on a rimmed baking sheet, then place the peeled sweetbreads on the paper towel. Cover with a second double thickness of paper towels and a second baking sheet, then place a can or other weight on top of the baking sheet. Transfer to the refrigerator and let stand overnight. The following day, bring the veal stock to a simmer in a saucepan. Add the pressed sweetbreads and poach for 30 minutes. Remove from the heat and let cool in the stock. When fully cool, cut the sweetbreads into ½-in/12-mm cubes.

3. Place the veal meat on a rimmed baking sheet, transfer to the freezer, and chill until crunchy on the exterior but not frozen solid (see page 23).

4. In a small bowl, add the egg, milk powder, cream, salt, fines herbes, and Cure No. 1 and stir to combine.

5. Nest a large mixing bowl in a bowl filled with ice. Grind the veal meat and the crushed ice, adding the ice a spoonful at a time as the mixture passes through the small die of the grinder into the bowl set in ice (see page 24).

6. Add the milk mixture to the meat and stir with your hands until well incorporated; the mixture will look homogenous and will begin sticking to the bowl (see page 25).

7. Spoon 2 tbsp of the meat mixture into a nonstick frying pan and spread into a thin patty. Cook the test patty over low heat until cooked through but not browned. Taste the sausage for seasoning and adjust as necessary. Transfer the farce to the refrigerator while you prepare the morels.

8. In a small sauté pan over high heat, heat the olive oil. When the oil is hot, add the morels and cook, stirring, for 2 minutes, then add the vermouth, reduce the heat to medium-low, and cook until the liquid has disappeared and the morels are tender, about 3 minutes longer. Remove the pan from the heat and set aside until completely cooled.

9. Remove the farce from the refrigerator and gently fold in the cubed sweetbreads and the morels. Press a sheet of parchment paper or plastic wrap directly on the surface of the meat to prevent oxidation, then cover the bowl tightly with plastic wrap and refrigerate overnight. Alternatively, you can vacuum-seal the farce.

CONTINUED

10. Preheat the oven to 350°F/180°C. Roll the pastry into a large rectangle about ⅛ in/3 mm thick. Using a 3-lb-/1.4-kg-capacity and 12-by-3-by-3¼-in/30.5-by-7.5-by-8-cm hinged pâté mold or similar terrine mold to guide you, cut the pastry to fit the mold with about ½ in/12 mm of overhang on all sides; cut one piece of dough to form the lid. Use a small round pastry cutter to cut two holes in the lid piece.

11. Lightly butter the inside of the terrine mold, then transfer the dough carefully to the mold and gently press so that the dough adheres to the sides of the terrine mold; if necessary, patch any holes or corners. Trim the overhang so that it's even on all sides.

12. Spoon the meat mixture into the dough-lined terrine mold, smoothing the top, then bang the mold on the work surface to eliminate air bubbles. Fold the dough overhang over the top of the terrine to begin to form the lid, pressing gently.

13. Brush the dough on the top of the terrine with some of the egg wash. Lay the lid piece of dough on top of the terrine, pressing gently so that it adheres to the egg-washed pastry beneath. Press any overhanging edges down inside the mold.

14. Cut two pieces of foil into rectangles, about 6 in/15 cm long by 4 in/10 cm wide. Fold each rectangle in half lengthwise, then roll into a tube. Place one tube in each of the holes that you have cut in the surface of the terrine; this will allow steam and juices to escape without marring the surface of the terrine.

15. Brush the entire surface of the pastry lid with the remaining egg wash, then transfer the terrine to the oven and bake for 1 hour 15 minutes, or until the terrine reaches an internal temperature of 145°F/63°C (insert the thermometer in one of the chimneys to check) and the top is nicely browned.

16. Remove from the oven and let stand at room temperature for 30 minutes. Transfer to the refrigerator and chill for at least 8 hours or overnight.

17. The next day, soak the gelatin sheet in cold water for 5 to 10 minutes. Gently heat the Madeira in a small saucepan over low heat (do not let it boil), then wring out the gelatin sheet and add to the Madeira, stirring until completely dissolved. Remove from the heat and let the mixture cool slightly. Remove the terrine from the refrigerator and carefully pour the Madeira through the chimneys, dividing evenly. Return the terrine to the refrigerator and refrigerate overnight. When you're ready to serve the terrine, carefully unmold it on a cutting board and cut with a sharp knife into thin slices.

CHAPTER 7

CONDIMENTS, BISCUITS, AND BUNS

biscuits ↘

catsup

beer mustard

pickled jalapeños

anchovy and mustard aioli

Every sausage in this book is flavorful enough to be eaten on its own, with no accompaniment. But what fun is that? This chapter features all the things that go on a good sausage, including catsup, beer mustard, and sauerkraut; the things that go alongside a good sausage, like a big green salad dressed with our lemon vinaigrette and spicy coleslaw; and vehicles for sausage, such as buns (of course) and buttery biscuits.

In a pinch, a store-bought condiment, side dish, or bun is just fine. But if you're challenging yourself to make exceptional sausages, you may as well go the extra mile and make the rest from scratch, too.

ANCHOVY AND MUSTARD AIOLI

....

YIELD: 2 CUPS/455 G

	U.S. MEASUREMENT	GRAMS	% OF TOTAL (100%)
Egg yolks	4	80	17.50
Minced anchovy fillets	¼ cup	43	9.50
Pickled Jalapeño liquid (see page 190) or water	1 tbsp	44	9.65
Whole-grain mustard	1 tbsp	18	4.00
Freshly ground black pepper	¼ tsp	2	0.40
Fine sea salt	1 tsp	7	1.50
Extra-virgin olive oil	⅔ cup	248	54.55
Finely chopped fresh parsley	2 tbsp	13	2.90

Even if you think that you don't like the flavor of anchovies, I'd like you to try making this aioli at least once. Balanced by the addition of whole-grain mustard and brightened by parsley, the anchovies add a deep savory flavor to the mayonnaise but the aioli isn't fishy. I like to spread this on sausages instead of mayonnaise or catsup.

1. In a medium nonreactive bowl, add the egg yolks, anchovy fillets, pickled jalapeño liquid, mustard, black pepper, and salt and whisk to combine.

2. Whisking continuously, add the olive oil, drop by drop at first, until the mixture begins to emulsify, then continue adding the oil in a thin, steady stream until it is all incorporated and the mixture is thick and creamy.

3. Whisk in the parsley. (Season with additional salt and pepper.) Use immediately, or transfer to a lidded container and refrigerate. The aioli will keep, refrigerated, for 2 days.

BEER MUSTARD

....

YIELD: 2 CUPS/455 G

	U.S. MEASUREMENT	GRAMS	% OF TOTAL (100%)
White vinegar	½ cup	133	29.20
Beer, such as pale ale	⅓ cup	88	19.47
Water	⅓ cup	87	19.21
Brown mustard seeds	1 cup	61	13.37
Sugar	2 tbsp	31	6.72
Dry mustard powder	¼ cup	22	4.80
Fine sea salt	1 tbsp	22	4.80
Ground coriander	1 tbsp + 1½ tsp	11	2.43

A smear of this spicy mustard is great on so many of the sausages in this book, including, of course, hot dogs. I like to use a hoppy pale ale beer in this recipe, because you can really taste its flavor in the finished mustard, but any type of lighter-bodied beer will work.

1. In a large-lidded nonreactive container, whisk together the vinegar, beer, water, and mustard seeds. Cover and refrigerate for 1 week.

2. Transfer the mustard seed mixture to a food processor and add the sugar, mustard powder, salt, and ground coriander and process until the mustard seeds have broken up. If you prefer a smoother texture, you can continue processing until the mustard reaches the desired consistency.

3. Transfer the mustard to a glass jar. Cover and refrigerate for a week before serving. The mustard will keep, refrigerated, for several months.

CATSUP

YIELD: 2 CUPS/455 G

	U.S. MEASUREMENT	GRAMS	% OF TOTAL (100%)
White vinegar	¼ cup	23	4.36
Water	½ cup	52	9.85
Paprika	½ cup	38	7.20
Dry mustard powder	¼ cup	9	1.61
Fine sea salt	2¼ tsp	8	1.42
Freshly ground black pepper	1 tbsp	4	0.76
Onion powder	2¼ tsp	3	0.57
Chili powder	4 tsp	5	0.95
Ground cumin	¾ tsp	2	0.27
Worcestershire	1½ tbsp	19	3.60
Honey	¼ cup	79	14.96
Canned whole tomatoes, chopped, with liquid	2 cups	288	54.45

Most commercial catsup is loaded with corn syrup and doesn't really taste like tomatoes at all. This version, which is sweetened with honey and loaded with spices, is our idea of what the classic condiment *ought* to taste like.

1. In a large saucepan, combine the vinegar, water, paprika, mustard powder, salt, black pepper, onion powder, chili powder, cumin, Worcestershire, honey, and tomatoes with their liquid. Bring to a boil over medium-high heat, then reduce the heat until the mixture is gently simmering. Cover and simmer for 1 hour, stirring occasionally, until the mixture has cooked down by about one-third. Remove from the heat and let cool slightly.

2. Pulse in a food processor (in batches if necessary) until smooth, then pass through a fine-mesh sieve. Let cool, then spoon into sterilized jars and refrigerate. The catsup will keep, refrigerated, for several months.

CHIMICHURRI

YIELD: 2 CUPS/455 G

	U.S. MEASUREMENT	GRAMS	% OF TOTAL (100%)
Hot water	¼ cup	59	13.06
Finely minced garlic cloves	¼ cup	40	8.78
Champagne vinegar	2 tbsp	30	6.64
Finely chopped fresh parsley	½ cup	27	6.00
Red pepper flakes	¼ cup	15	3.21
Lemon zest	1 tbsp	10	2.14
Fine sea salt	¾ tsp	6	1.28
Paprika	¾ tsp	6	1.28
Finely chopped fresh oregano	¾ tsp	4	0.86
Extra-virgin olive oil	⅔ cup	258	56.75

This herb salsa recipe is inspired by one in Francis Mallmann's spectacular grilling book *Seven Fires*. It has a bright, tangy, spicy flavor and is an excellent foil for rich grilled meats, including sausages. I like to make the chimichurri a day or two before I plan to serve it, which allows the flavors to mellow and combine. I love serving this with the Chicken and Egg Galantine (page 136).

1. In a medium bowl, whisk together the water, garlic, vinegar, parsley, red pepper flakes, lemon zest, salt, paprika, and oregano and stir to combine. Gradually whisk in the olive oil.

2. Transfer to a lidded glass jar, cover, and refrigerate for 2 days before using. The chimichurri is best used within 2 weeks.

CARAMELIZED ONIONS

....

YIELD: 1 CUP/170 G

	U.S. MEASUREMENT	GRAMS	% OF TOTAL (100%)
Unsalted butter	2 tbsp	30	2.46
Medium onions, peeled, halved, and thinly sliced	2	454	97.01
Fine sea salt	½ tsp	3	0.32
Freshly ground black pepper	¼ tsp	2	0.21

These sweet-and-sticky onions make a fantastic topping for sausages, burgers, and grilled cheese sandwiches. Though they take about an hour to make, they require very little attention.

1. Heat the butter in a large skillet over medium-high heat. When the butter is melted and starts to brown, add the onions and let cook, without stirring, for the first 2 to 3 minutes. Once the onions on the bottom layer have begun to brown, season with the salt and pepper, stir, and reduce the heat to low. Let cook, stirring occasionally until all onions have a rich golden brown color and are soft and sweet to the taste, about 1 hour.

2. Serve warm or transfer to an airtight container and store in the refrigerator for up to 1 week. Let come to room temperature before using.

GARLIC CONFIT

....

YIELD: 2 CUPS/455 G

	U.S. MEASUREMENT	GRAMS	% OF TOTAL (100%)
Garlic cloves, peeled	1½ cups	209	46.14
Extra-virgin olive oil	⅔ cup	209	46.14
Fresh thyme leaves	¼ cup	9	2.03
Fine sea salt	1 tbsp	21	4.67
Coarsely ground black pepper	1½ tsp	5	1.02

Cooking garlic cloves slowly in olive oil yields two excellent ingredients: soft, sweet cloves of garlic, which can be spread on bread, added to roasted vegetables, or used in sausage farce, as well as garlic oil. Cook sausages in the fragrant oil, or use it to dress raw or cooked vegetables.

1. In a medium saucepan over low heat, combine the garlic, olive oil, thyme, salt, and black pepper. Cook the garlic until the tip of a knife slips easily into the cloves, about 1 hour. If the garlic begins to brown before the cloves are soft, reduce the heat.

2. Remove the pan from the heat and let cool slightly, then transfer the garlic and oil to a lidded glass jar and refrigerate until ready to use, for up to 2 weeks. Let it come to room temperature before using.

HARISSA

YIELD: 2 CUPS/455 G

	U.S. MEASUREMENT	GRAMS	% OF TOTAL (100%)
Fine sea salt	½ cup	170	37.42
Ancho chile powder	½ cup	45	9.81
Granulated garlic	⅓ cup	35	7.60
Paprika	⅓ cup	30	6.69
Cayenne pepper	⅓ cup	28	6.13
Sugar	1 tbsp	28	6.13
Coriander seeds, finely ground	1 tbsp	23	5.15
Cumin seeds, finely ground	1 tbsp	19	4.22
Coarsely ground black pepper	1 tbsp	19	4.17
Chipotle powder	1 tbsp	17	3.68
Caraway seeds, coarsely ground	1 tbsp	16	3.49
Red pepper flakes	1½ tsp	13	2.82
Fennel seeds, coarsely ground	1½ tsp	11	2.44
Dry spearmint	1½ tsp	1	0.25

For years I relied on another company's harissa spice blend to make my Merguez (page 62). The price of the blend crept up over the years until it reached nearly $45 a pound; that was when I decided to make my own. Unlike the prepared harissa that you typically find at the store, this is a dry spice blend. I use it in combination with tomato paste in the merguez, but it can be mixed with olive oil to form a paste that can then be rubbed on chicken or pork before cooking.

1. In a medium bowl, whisk together the salt, ancho chile powder, granulated garlic, paprika, cayenne, sugar, coriander seeds, cumin seeds, black pepper, chipotle powder, caraway seeds, red pepper flakes, fennel seeds, and spearmint.

2. Transfer to a lidded glass jar. The spice blend will keep indefinitely, but is best used within a few months.

HORSERADISH AND BLACK PEPPER CREMA

YIELD: 2 CUPS/480 ML

	U.S. MEASUREMENT	GRAMS	% OF TOTAL (100%)
Sour cream	2 cups	288	63.54
Freshly grated horseradish	⅔ cup	51	11.24
Finely chopped fresh parsley	1 cup	39	8.65
Heavy cream	⅓ cup	35	7.64
Water	2 tbsp	20	4.32
Fine sea salt	2 tsp	7	1.59
Lemon zest	2 tsp	7	1.44
Lemon juice	1 tbsp	5	1.15
Freshly ground black pepper	1 tsp	2	0.43

Beef and horseradish are a classic pairing, and I like spreading this condiment on any of the beef or lamb sausages in the book. Freshly grated horseradish root has an appealing nose-clearing quality and is much more pungent than the jars of pre-grated stuff you find at the grocery store, so use that if you can find it.

1. In a medium bowl, whisk together the sour cream, horseradish, parsley, heavy cream, water, salt, lemon zest, lemon juice, and black pepper. (Season with additional salt, lemon juice, or pepper, if desired.)

2. Transfer to a lidded container and refrigerate; it will keep for 1 week.

LEMON VINAIGRETTE

MAKES: 2 CUPS/480 ML

	U.S. MEASUREMENT	GRAMS	% OF TOTAL (100%)
Lemon juice	1 cup	222	49.00
Finely chopped fresh parsley leaves	¼ cup	13	2.90
Fine sea salt	2¼ tsp	7	1.60
Freshly ground black pepper	1 tsp	2	0.50
Extra-virgin olive oil	⅔ cup	209	46.00

This is the 4505 Meats "house dressing." I love serving sausages alongside a big green salad, using whatever seasonal greens are available at the farmers' market, and more often than not this is the dressing that I'll use. Invest in a bottle of good-quality olive oil and use it here—you'll taste the difference.

1. In a medium bowl, add the lemon juice, parsley, salt, and black pepper and whisk to combine. Very slowly drizzle in the olive oil, whisking continuously, until it has all been incorporated and the dressing looks emulsified. (Season with additional salt and pepper, if desired.)

2. The dressing will keep in a lidded jar in the refrigerator for 3 days; let it come to room temperature before using.

PICKLED JALAPEÑOS

. . . .

YIELD: 2 CUPS/455 G

	U.S. MEASUREMENT	GRAMS	% OF TOTAL (100%)
Fresh jalapeño chiles, sliced into ⅛-in-/ 3-mm-thick rings	0.85 lb	192	42.34
White vinegar	1 cup	119	26.29
Water	1 cup	119	26.28
Sugar	2 tbsp	14	3.18
Fine sea salt	2¼ tsp	9	1.91

I'm kind of addicted to pickling, and I use this basic brine to pickle tons of vegetables, from carrots to onions to chiles. The chiles are an awesome burger and sausage topping and a key ingredient in our Spicy Slaw (page 194).

1. Place the jalapeño chiles in a 1-quart-/1-liter-size glass jar. In a medium nonreactive saucepan, combine the vinegar, water, sugar, and salt. Bring to a simmer, stirring until the sugar is dissolved, then remove from the heat and let stand for 30 minutes.

2. Pour the liquid over the chiles and let cool completely. Cover the jar and refrigerate for 2 weeks before using.

VARIATIONS

This recipe can also be used for shallots or red onions, as well as carrots, cauliflower, and radishes. Thinly slice all vegetables before pickling them. Shallots and red onions will be ready in as little as 3 hours, while the heartier vegetables should sit in the pickling liquid for 2 weeks.

SAUERKRAUT

YIELD: 10 CUPS/2.3 KG

	U.S. MEASUREMENT	GRAMS	% OF TOTAL (100%)
Finely shredded green cabbage	5.00 lb	2,268	97.30
Fine sea salt	3 tbsp	57	2.50
Caraway seeds	2¼ tsp	5	0.20

Sauerkraut is a sausage's best friend. I love the flavor of this naturally fermented version, which develops gradually over its three-week maturation period. During that time the sauerkraut becomes tart and funky but retains its crunch, which I believe is a key attribute of a good kraut. This makes a big batch, but it goes fast. While it's terrific on a grilled sausage, it's also the foundation of French *choucroute garnie* and is mighty tasty added to a grilled cheese sandwich.

1. In a large plastic or ceramic container, combine the cabbage, salt, and caraway seeds and mix well with your hands. Cover tightly and let stand at warm room temperature (about 75°F/24°C; if your kitchen is cool, you can put it on top of your refrigerator) until the mixture begins to release liquid, about 2 days.

2. Transfer to an electric stand mixer fitted with the paddle attachment and mix on medium speed for 2 minutes until more juices (brine) have been released. Pack the cabbage into five pint-size canning jars, making sure brine covers the cabbage by at least 1 in/2.5 cm and leaving 1 in/2.5 cm to 2 in/5 cm of space at the top.

3. Let the jars stand in a cool, dark place (approximately 65°F/18°C to 70°F/21°C) for 5 days. Slowly open and quickly close jars to gently release built-up pressure, being careful not to let the liquid bubble out. Let stand for 5 days longer. Reopen jars to release pressure.

4. Let stand for 5 days longer (for a total of 15 days), then taste to determine if the kraut is sour enough. Let stand until the kraut is to your liking, continuing to open the jars every few days to release pressure. When the sauerkraut is as sour as you like it, transfer the jars to the refrigerator. The kraut will continue to ferment, but slowly. Open the containers periodically to release gas; the sauerkraut will keep, refrigerated, for 3 months.

SPICY SLAW

....

YIELD: 4 CUPS/910 G

	U.S. MEASUREMENT	GRAMS	% OF TOTAL (100%)
Shredded green cabbage	5 cups	650	71.54
Pickled Jalapeños (page 190)	¼ cup	29	3.16
Pickled Jalapeño liquid (see page 190)	⅓ cup	86	9.47
Pickled carrots (see page 191, variation)	¼ cup	29	3.16
Pickled red onion (see page 191, variation)	¼ cup	29	3.16
Thinly sliced raw red onion	¼ cup	29	3.16
Finely chopped fresh cilantro	¼ cup	16	1.77
Fine sea salt	½ tsp	2	0.20
Extra-virgin olive oil	3 tbsp	40	4.40

Though I like coleslaw that is dressed with the standard sweet mayonnaise-based dressing, this spicy slaw is a lighter alternative. The method for making it is a bit different, too—I toss half of the cabbage with the pickled vegetables and pickling liquid and let it sit overnight so that it softens and absorbs that vinegary flavor, then stir in the remaining cabbage just before serving so that the finished slaw has crunch and body.

1. In a large bowl, add half of the cabbage, the pickled jalapeños, jalapeño pickling liquid, pickled carrots, pickled red onion, and raw red onion and stir well to combine. Cover with plastic wrap and let stand, refrigerated, overnight.

2. Just before serving, stir in the remaining cabbage, cilantro, salt, and olive oil and mix until well combined. (Season as desired with additional salt and coarsely ground black pepper.)

BISCUITS

YIELD: 12 BISCUITS

	U.S. MEASUREMENT	GRAMS	% OF TOTAL (100%)
Cake flour	5 cups	609	44.69
Baking powder	1 tbsp + ¼ tsp	24	1.78
Baking soda	1 tbsp + ¾ tsp	17	1.22
Salt	¾ tsp	8	0.56
Cold unsalted butter, cut into small cubes	0.50 lb + 1 tbsp	309	22.70
Buttermilk	1½ cups	396	29.05

An egg, sausage, and biscuit sandwich is one of the greatest ways to start the day. These flaky numbers are sturdy enough to hold up to the sandwich treatment, but light enough that they melt in your mouth. Split them and top them with patties of Maple-Bacon Breakfast Sausage (page 60) and a fried egg, or use them as the base for a killer batch of biscuits and sausage gravy.

1. Preheat the oven to 415°F/212°C. In a large bowl, whisk together the flour, baking powder, baking soda, and salt. Using a pastry cutter or two knives, cut 0.50 lb/227 g of the butter into the dry ingredients until the mixture resembles coarse meal.

2. Turn the dry mixture out onto a lightly floured work surface and drizzle the buttermilk over. Using the tips of your fingers, incorporate the buttermilk into the dry ingredients, taking care not to overwork the mixture. The dough will be wet but should not be sticky. Press the dough into a shaggy circle. Using a lightly floured rolling pin, roll the dough out to ½ in/12 mm thick. Using a 2¼-in/5.5-cm round cutter, cut out the biscuits as close as possible. Gather the dough scraps and knead together, then roll the dough out again and cut out additional biscuits. Discard any remaining scraps.

3. Arrange the biscuits, sides touching, on an ungreased baking sheet. Melt the remaining 1 tbsp butter, then brush the top of each biscuit with melted butter. Bake until golden brown, 10 to 12 minutes.

4. Transfer to a cooling rack. Serve warm or at room temperature.

HOT DOG BUNS

....

YIELD: 18 BUNS

	U.S. MEASUREMENT	GRAMS	% OF TOTAL (100%)
Sugar	¼ cup	60	4.50
Instant dry yeast	1 tsp	9	0.70
Warm water	½ cup	122	9.00
Warm whole milk (95ºF/35ºC to 105ºF/40ºC)	2¼ cups	488	36.00
Fine sea salt	3 tsp	12	1.00
All-purpose flour	5 cups	620	45.50
Egg wash (1 egg yolk beaten with 1 tsp water)	—	—	—
Sesame seeds (preferably a mixture of black and white)	¼ cup	45	3.30

Soft, squishy, and slightly sweet, these tender buns are perfect for any of the sausages in this book. They are best eaten freshly baked.

1. In a bowl of an electric mixer fitted with the dough hook attachment, dissolve the sugar and yeast in the warm water and let stand for 5 minutes. Add the milk, salt, and 2½ cups/300 g of the flour to the mixer and mix on medium speed for 3 minutes. (This can also be done in a large bowl; mix the dough vigorously with a wooden spoon.)

2. Reduce the mixer speed to low and add in the remaining flour, ¼ cup/30 g at a time, until the dough begins to pull away from the sides of the bowl. When all the flour has been incorporated, increase the mixer speed to medium and mix for 5 minutes, until you have a smooth, elastic dough. The dough will be quite soft and sticky.

3. Place the dough into a large oiled bowl, turning once to coat entirely with oil. Cover with a clean, damp kitchen towel and let rise in a warm place until doubled, 45 minutes to 1 hour.

4. Punch down the dough, then turn out onto a floured work surface and let it rest, covered, overnight. The next day, divide the dough into three pieces, then each piece into six, so you have a total of eighteen equal pieces. Roll each piece into a ball, then roll the balls into 6-in-/15-cm-long logs. Press each log gently with your hand to flatten it slightly, then transfer to two baking sheets (nine buns per sheet), spacing the buns about ½ in/12 mm apart. Cover the pans loosely with plastic wrap and let rise in a warm place until nearly doubled, about 45 minutes.

5. Preheat the oven to 375°F/190°C. Brush the egg wash on the top of each bun and sprinkle with the sesame seeds, then transfer to the oven and bake for 20 minutes. Remove the buns from the baking sheet and let cool on a wire rack. The buns will keep for a few days but are best the day they are made.

RESOURCES

SAUSAGE-MAKING EQUIPMENT
K. Doving, San Francisco, California
Contact by phone only: 415-861-6694

CASINGS, CURE SALTS, AND OTHER SAUSAGE-MAKING EQUIPMENT
Butcher and Packer, Madison Heights, Wisconsin
www.butcher-packer.com

FOIE GRAS
D'Artagnan, Newark, New Jersey
www.dartagnan.com

MAIL-ORDER SAUSAGE
4505 Meats, San Francisco, California
4505meats.com

SAUSAGE STUFFERS AND KNIVES
F. Dick, Farmingdale, New York
www.dick.de/en

SMOKERS
Southern Pride, Alamo, Tennessee
www.southern-pride.com

WOOD-BURNING GRILLS
Grillworks, Washington, DC
www.grillery.com

INDEX